No Rights and No RESPECT

a
Documentary
COMMENTARY
On AFRICAN LIFE in AMERICA
by
Pastor Michael S. Williams, D.Min.

Resource *Publications*

An imprint of *Wipf and Stock Publishers*
150 West Broadway • Eugene OR 97401

The Juneteenth Publishing Group
San Francisco, CA

Published and Printed in the United States of America

© Pastor Michael S. Williams, D.Min. 2000

All rights reserved. No part of this publication may be reproduced, stored in a retrieval system, or transmitted, in any form or by any means, electronic, mechanical, photocopying, recording, or otherwise without the prior permission of The Juneteenth Publishing Group.

This book is sold subject to the condition that it shall not, by way of trade or otherwise, be lent, re-sold, hired out or otherwise circulated without the publisher's prior consent in any form of binding or cover other than that in which it is published and without a similar condition including this condition being imposed upon the subsequent publisher.

Resource Publications
An imprint of *Wipf and Stock Publishers*
150 West Broadway
Eugene, Oregon 97401

No Rights and No Respect
A Documentary Commentary on African Life in America
By Williams, Michael S.
©2001 Williams, Michael S.
ISBN: 1-57910-669-2
Publication Date: June, 2001

**The Juneteenth Publishing Group
San Francisco, California**

This BOOK is intended for CIVIL COMMENTARY purposes *only*. It is an expression of the author's First Amendment rights, *should they actually exist*, under the **United States Constitution**. It is sold with the understanding that neither the publisher nor the author are engaged in the profession of providing advice in any manner, including, but not limited to: relationship counseling, therapy, psychological counseling, medicine, law, or any other manner of advice. **NOTHING** in this **BOOK** is intended to suggest an altering of the political establishment of the United States of America. If treasonous intent is read into this book, it will be done on *Constitutional* grounds. In other words, treasonous intent will be manipulated from this book so as to pay for the luxurious lifestyle of Federal Agents, Marshals, Court Clerks, Judges, etc. They have and will always thrive at the expense of **AFRICAN** people.

Third Printing
The Juneteenth Publishing Group
San Francisco, CA

E-Mail Address: PMSW46@aol.com

Table of Contents

Foreword 9

Introduction 13

The Declaration of Independence (1776) 25

Excerpts From Thomas Jefferson's *Notes on the State of Virginia* (1781-1782) 37

Mr. James Madison's Notes on the SLAVERY Debate at the Constitutional Convention (Tuesday, August 22, 1787) 40

Excerpts From The United States Constitution (1787) 48

The Fugitive Slave Act of 1850 63

The United States Supreme Court's Dred Scott Decision (1856) 77

Abraham Lincoln On The Dred Scott Decision (1857) 138

The Emancipation Proclamation (1863) 160

40 Acres and A Mule (1865) 170

The Freedman's Bureau Act of 1865 177

Amendments 13-15 of the Constitution 1865-68 183

Conclusion 188

Appendices 192

Appendix A 193

Appendix B 200

Appendix C 203

Appendix D 206

Appendix E 207

Appendix F 209

Appendix G 215

About the Author 217

Published Writings by Dr. Williams 218

To Patricia Ann

Exodus 14:14

"[AFRICANS] are altogether unfit to associate with the white race, either in social or political relations; and so far inferior, that they had no rights which the white man was bound to respect..."

Roger Brooke Taney
United States Chief Justice of the Supreme Court
1857

Foreword

In his previous book, *From Eden to Egypt: The Book of Genesis Revisited*,[1] Dr. Michael S. Williams fulfilled the role of African-Centric reclamation scholar/preacher/prophet. He meticulously illustrated on a literary tapestry the reclamation of African contributions to the peoples and religions of the ancient so-called Middle East, with particular attention to Judaism and Christianity. Dr. Williams carefully gathered and organized the facts and presented them in a very convincing straightforward literary style. I have had the privilege of reading several books on the subject, but this statement of Dr. Williams, which is substantiated by a plethora of solid facts, is one of the best yet. If you have not read this book, please try and secure a copy; it is must reading for those of you who would like to know about the role **AFRICANS** played in the formation of the Christian religion most of us adhere to in the United States.

In this present publication, Dr. Williams dons the role of prophetic insurrectionist, as he unearths and presents suppressed

---

[1] Pastor Michael S. Williams, D.Min. *From Eden to Egypt: the Book of Genesis Revisited* (San Francisco: The Juneteenth Publishing Group, 1999).

information and therefore attempts to alter the reader's traditional beliefs about the **United States Constitution** and its relationship to African Americans.

Dr. Williams takes the reader on a journey to the past by examining historical documents and bringing them to life as he skillfully weaves them into a literary form that is readily understood. This is an important work concerning liberation, and that is what it is, because he is attempting on a seminal level to change our traditional understanding about our "protection" and "guarantees" under the **United States Constitution**.

In his analysis of the Constitution he depicts a "sacrosanct" document held by all white men to be the most perfect attempt at recognition and protection of the rights of all men as a piece of paper that in reality promises the African American nothing but grief. He proves that the enslaved **AFRICANS** were not even considered in the phrase, "We the people!" They were considered property and had no rights in light of the Constitution! He draws from several historical documents to support his point.

He illustrates how the Constitution is written in such a way that, at times, the Supreme Court must interpret its intent, and depending on the ideology of the Court, a corresponding decision is rendered. At times, the mood of white folk has influenced the interpretation; at other times, the black/white political situation.

His material begs the question of possible collusion, at least in ideology, of the slave codes and the Constitution. This question is begged in lieu of the fact of the Constitution being the law of the land and no state can make laws that are contrary to the "laws of the land." Why were the slave codes legal? They were legal because they did not apply to the citizens, "We the people," but to *property owned by the citizens.*

This book will open the blindest eye, if it is read and understood. It offers an answer to many of the questions we raise about why there is a proverbial playing field in which we must participate and we must always be downhill at a 75-degree angle.

This is a book you will either cherish or despise for the new perspective on the problem of the African in the United States.

If you are an African American, this is a book you *must* read.

Rev John D Brinson, M/Div.

George Washington
1732-1799
Native Virginian
Father of *His* Country
Commanding General of Colonial Army
Slave Holder
Chaired Constitutional Convention (1787)
First President of the United States (1789-1797)

Introduction

The late **AFRICAN**[1] writer/social commentator, Richard Wright (1908-1960) once mused, "expression springs out of an environment."[2] If that were the case, a society, specifically American society, can be judged by its "sacred" texts. These documents, as I will seek to show, provide the necessary "legal" reference points that "prove" **AFRICAN** "inferiority." They provide the legal wherewithal needed to either *grant* or *withhold* **AFRICAN** participation in the American experience.

---

[1] Anyone familiar with my writing slant knows that I am of the opinion that persons of African descent can never "do" enough to be allowed full participation in the American experience; therefore I do not consider them to be "Americans." I do not consider myself an "American." I will refer to them throughout this book as "Africans." This is not a very farfetched proposition. African **SLAVES** arriving in America's British colonies in the Seventeenth and Eighteenth Centuries were well aware of their "inferior" status. Therefore, they made it a point to acknowledge their unique heritage. They called themselves "Africans." Campbell notes that persons of African descent in this country, up until the mid-1820s and late 1830s, referred to themselves as "Africans," because the term "**Negro**" was equated with "**SLAVE**." Hence, most Black institutions contained the word "African," in their title, e.g., The *African* Free Lodge, The *African* Methodist Episcopal Church, The Free *African* Society, etc. The name fell into disuse by the 1830s due to attempts on the part of powerful interests in the United States that sought to deport *all "free"* blacks to Africa. James T. Campbell, *Songs of Zion: The African Methodist Episcopal Church in the United States and South Africa* (New York: Oxford University Press, 1995), vii, 73. Also, Richard B. Moore, *The Name "**Negro**," Its Origin and Evil Use*, ed., W. Burghart Turner and Joyce Moore-Turner (Baltimore: Black Classics Press, 1992), 62.

[2] Richard Wright, *White Man Listen!* (New York: Doubleday 1964), 83.

What's that I hear? I believe I hear a rising chorus of "protest" coming from the "Big House" where Massa and the "House Negroes"[3] reside! I believe I hear them caucusing and strategizing! Here it comes! The tired lines relating to "we're not perfect, but over the last two centuries, we've made progress!" "Look over there! High ranking military **Negroes**! **Negroes** with (in) security clearances! **Negroes** in Congress! **Negroes** sitting on local, state, and federal benches! They even get to wear black robes! Read your own magazines! Look at all the **Negro** 'firsts!' An **African** even serves as Secretary of State."

On a superficial level, the protest is correct! The protestors have every reason and right to criticize my assertion! But even their criticism falls flat in the face of the **AFRICANS** that are literally walking wounded! An ever-rising chorus of wounded souls cries out with the pathetic wails of the deceived! Deceived? Yes! Deceived! They thought that doing the right

---

[3] The term "**Negro**" has historically been equated with the term "**SLAVE**." James T. Campbell, *Songs of Zion: The African Methodist Episcopal Church in the United States and South Africa* (New York: Oxford University Press, 1995), vii, 73. Also, Richard B. Moore, *The Name "Negro," Its Origin and Evil Use*, ed., W. Burghart Turner and Joyce Moore-Turner (Baltimore: Black Classics Press, 1992), 62. There were/are two types of **SLAVES**, the "House **Negro**" and the "Field **Negro**." The House **SLAVE** looked upon himself as occupying a privileged position. S/he may have even been the result of the union between a female **SLAVE** and Massa. In any case, even though s/he got to suck the meatless bones scavenged from Massa's garbage can, wear Massa's cast off clothes, serve as an informant as to what the other **SLAVES** were doing, s/he was still a **SLAVE**! The "Field" **SLAVE** suffered under no such illusions. The "Field" **SLAVE** had one goal—**SURVIVAL**! Survival meant either running away, staging work slow downs, or even destroying crops or property! America is still a huge plantation! Africans in America are still considered **SLAVES**!

"thing" would grant that elusive experience they sought—*equality* with *real* (Euro) Americans! They thought if they went to the *right* schools, married a person with the *correct* skin tone, joined the *right* clubs and political party, fought in America's wars (against colored peoples no less!), *picked* enough cotton, *forged* enough steel, *arrested* enough of their fellow **AFRICANS**, *infiltrated* enough **AFRICAN** groups and *shined* enough shoes—they would be granted that elusive quality they so desperately sought (dare I say **EURO-AMERICANNESS?)** equality!

During their earlier years, they might have cried out in smugness, "we don't need affirmative action, all we need is a fair chance!" But alas to the last man and woman, they found out that regardless of their "achievements" in ways that were unique professionally to their situation, they were still "**SLAVES!**[4]"

---

[4] To the many "**Negroes**" that will protest my views; I invite my misguided brothers and sisters to review the works of the walking wounded and/or disillusioned persons of African descent. I will list a few. Paul M. Barrnett, *The Good Black: A True Story of Race in America*, (New York: E.P. Hutton, 1999), Joseph Jett, *Black and White on Wall Street: The Untold Story of the Man Wrongly Accused of Bringing Down Kidder Peabody* (New York: William Morrow and Company, Inc., 1999), Howard L. Wallace, *Federal Plantation: Affirmative (In) Action Within Our Federal Government* (Edgewood, MD: Duncan & Duncan Publishers, Inc. 1996) and Tyrone Power's *Eyes to My Soul: The Rise or Decline of a Black FBI Agent* (Dover, MA: The Majority Press). Bruce Wright, *Black Robes, White Justice: Why Our Legal System Doesn't Work for Blacks* (New York: Carol Publishing Group, 1994). African Secret Service Agents are currently locked in a legal battle with their agency, the US Secret Service. In their class action suit, they are alleging discrimination in promotional opportunities, and professional advancement. African FBI Agents just concluded a protracted 10-year battle in Federal court alleging grievances similar to those of the African Secret

Alas my poor deluded brothers and sisters! If you are a judge, congressperson, military officer, millionaire, university official (at a **EURO-AMERICAN** university no less!) you are only in that position because the Euro-American people in charge thought that it was "time" for a **An African**! If those positions can be *given* –they can also be *taken away*! By extension, if the "laws" that "guarantee" **AFRICAN** "rights" can be *passed*, they can also be *withdrawn*! The occupant of the nation's highest office, the presidency, has always been identifiably *Euro-American*, the majority of the employees of the Federal Executive Branch of government, both civil servant and appointee, are *Euro-American*. The majority of all judges are *Euro-American*. There is no legislative body of consequence in this nation with an **AFRICAN** majority! If there are **AFRICAN** members of these institutions, especially the judiciary and the legislature, national or state, it is *only because the majority has deemed it the right time to allow AN AFRICAN into its ranks*! After his/her purpose has been fulfilled, they become expendable!

It is this understanding of **AFRICAN** life in America that caused the great **AFRICAN** historian, Carter G. Woodson (1875-1950), founder of the Association for the Study of Negro Life and History, to remark in 1921,

---

Service Agents. But even this "victory" has been qualified by the fact that a special panel must consider their complaints!

> *The citizenship of the [AFRICAN] in this country is a fiction.* The Constitution of the United States guarantees to him every right vouchsafed to any individual by the most liberal democracy on the face of the earth [!]...but despite the unusual powers of the Federal Government, this agent of the body politic has studiously evaded the duty of safe guarding the rights of the **[AFRICAN]** {Italics Added}[5]

How did/do brilliant, as well as not so intelligent, persons of **AFRICAN** descent come to such dubious conclusions concerning their "equality?" How can they miss what so many observant **AFRICANS**, such as Woodson saw? They came to such mind altering and shocking conclusions because they read everything but America's "Sacred Texts." If they do read the texts, they read them out of "context." In other words, they do not look at the historical circumstances that made such documents possible and necessary! What are those texts? They range in the millions! Time and spatial concerns will not allow me to list and comment upon all of them. I selected a few of the most famous, as well as not so famous, writings for comment and reflection produced by the "American" experience.[6] Some

---

[5] Carter G. Woodson, "Fifty Years of **Negro** Citizenship as Qualified by the United States Supreme Court," *Journal of Negro History* 6:1 (January 1921):1.

[6] The proper noun "America" means in its exactitude the entire Western Hemisphere (North America, Mexico, Central and South America, inclusive of the Caribbean Islands). When I speak of "America," I mean the 48 contiguous states situated between Canada and Mexico, along with the state of Alaska. "America," is inclusive of its so-called "possessions," i.e., American Samoa, Puerto Rico, the

of the selected documents carry no "legal" force.⁷ In other words, they are not formally referenced when it comes to adjudicating the **AFRICAN'S** legal "status." But they are helpful in understanding the predatory, as well as cynical, foundational documents that *do* carry legal force.⁸ Even when the document *seemed* to favor **AFRICANS**, it was forced upon the American public with the implicit understanding that it would quietly be forgotten!⁹

In any case, none of the documents presented in this study were ever put in place with *any* significant **AFRICAN** participation! For instance, the debates surrounding the adoption of the American Constitution had absolutely no input from **AFRICAN** people! The document that arose from the Constitutional Convention, the **United States Constitution**, that

---

U.S. Virgin Islands, Guam, Wake Island, Midway, Micronesia, and the Northern Mariana Islands. By extension, anywhere "America" extends its social custom, attitudes concerning race, economic might/exploitation can also be considered "American" territory.

⁷ The Declaration of Independence, Jefferson's *Notes on the State of Virginia*d Madison's Constitutional Convention notes.

⁸ The United States Constitution, the **Fugitive Slave Act of 1850**, the Dred Scott Decision (1856), and **Amendments 13-15** to the Constitution (1865-68).

⁹ The Emancipation Proclamation (1863), Union Army General William T. Sherman's famous Special Field Order. No. 15 Headquarters Military Division of the Mississippi. In the Field, Savannah, Ga., January 16, 1865 which among other things promised freed African **SLAVES** "40 Acres and a Mule." (1865), and the Freedman's Bureau Act of 1865.

convened in Philadelphia[10] specifically termed persons of **AFRICAN** descent living in **SLAVERY** as being **3/5 human!**

Of course there are some **AFRICANS** that are under the delusion that their ancestors were part of the political process that brought this *"predastate"*[11] into existence. The present **AFRICAN** justice on the Supreme Court, Clarence Thomas, actually believes that he is a full participant in American democracy. The late **AFRICAN** Federal Appellate Judge, Justice William Higginbotham, Jr. had an interesting analysis of this poor misguided fellow. He said,

> My daughter suggests the following (she has a Ph.D. in clinical psychology.) She says Clarence Thomas must think that had he been living in 1776 he would have been a confidant of Thomas Jefferson, or if he were living in 1787, he would have been a confidant of James Madison....Thomas never considered that in all probability he would have been Jefferson's or Madison's *SLAVE*[!] We must always recognize the historic fact that despite all the good things Jefferson, Madison, and those others did; [**AFRICANS**] were in a status called *SLAVERY*

---

[10] The Convention convened at Philadelphia on May 5, 1787. It submitted a signed draft to Congress on September 17, 1787.

[11] The word "predastate" is a compound of the words "predator" and "state." America is a predatory state that has a parasitic relationship with the world in general but with Africans within its sphere of influence in particular. It exists for the sole purpose of eroding the humanity of any one that it considers inferior.

when the Constitution was drafted. [Italics Added]. [12]

At the risk of sounding cynical, but historically accurate, **AFRICANS** *did* play a decisive part in the formulation of the Declaration of Independence and the Federal Constitution! If you consider cleaning the Founding Father's spittoons, providing livery service (tending and cleaning up after the horses of George Washington, Thomas Jefferson, Benjamin Franklin, etc.), shining shoes, and laundering the clothes of the delegates that wrote the Declaration of Independence and the Constitution. In the case of the women, they may have been forced to provide sexual favors for the delegates!

My Audience and Aim

I am writing to **AFRICANS** that are classified as being *uniformed* and *unaware*. They are so unaware and uninformed that they think going to *jail and prison is normal*! They don't realize that their involvement in the Criminal (In) Justice System is nothing more than a plot to provide jobs and a comfortable lifestyle for their oppressors! [13]

---

[12] A. Leon Higginbotham, Jr. "Opening Argument," in Linn Washington, ed., *Black Judges on Justice: Perspectives from the Bench* (New York: The Free Press, 1994), 6.

[13] There are definite economic benefits to be realized by increasing the African male jail and prison population. After all, there is money to be made and jobs to be created with the construction of additional jails and prisons! There are support services that go along with imprisonment, i.e., uniforms for prisoners and guards, janitorial supplies, food for the inmates and staff. Concrete, barbed wire, electronic surveillance systems, tear gas, firearms, and pepper spray must be

Finally as an **AFRICAN** preacher, I realize that I have a choice. I can attempt to curry Massa's favor, or I can play the role the LORD of history assigned to all **AFRICAN** preachers whether they want to accept it or not! That role is to share the Gospel of Jesus Christ with all, but especially with the oppressed! Either way, as an **AFRICAN** preacher, I am automatically under suspicion, regardless as to if I understand myself as a "House" or a "Field" **SLAVE**.[14]

---

purchased. Imprisonment is more than locking a person up. It is a very profitable enterprise. Jerome G. Miller calls this process, "the Cold War of the 1990s." This "Cold War" of the 1990s has its own version of the Military-Industrial Complex. Miller calls it the "Crime Control-Industrial Complex." With the collapse of Communism, a need arose to continue expenditures that had formerly been directed against the Soviet Union. The Cold War had produced jobs and profits for defense contractors. It was a simple matter then for some of those same contractors to seek conversion of their technologies to domestic use. With their resources now directed towards a domestic market, the target population became, instead of Russians, African Americans, specifically males. The new idea was to warehouse them in high-tech prisons. There is now a great demand for prisons to be built in rural areas. This is due to the economic boom caused by prison construction as well as vending opportunities. This assists the local population economically as well as the contractors that profit by warehousing African Men in prison. Jerome G. Miller, *Search and Destroy: African-American Males in the Criminal Justice System* (Cambridge, UK: Cambridge University Press, 1996), 228, 230-231.

[14] African preachers led three of the most famous **SLAVE** revolts in the early 1800s. These preachers *interpreted* the **Old Testament** in such a way as to lead their followers to believe that God condemned their oppression as well as their oppressors. Those preachers were, Richmond, Virginia's Gabriel Prosser, (1802), Charleston, South Carolina's Denmark Vesey, (1822), and South Hampton, Virginia's Nat Turner, (1831) Gayraud Wilmore, *Black Religion and Black Radicalism: An Interpretation of the Religious History of Afro-American People* (Maryknoll, NY, 1991), 53-73. Revelations have surfaced over the last two decades which suggest the United States Government sees the African preacher as

A Plausible Constitutional Scenario

The **United States Constitution** is our nation's most **SACRED TEXT**. In its name, any thing, and I do mean any thing has/can be done!

The **United States Constitution** serves as the nation's legal template. Any law passed at any level of our national experience, whether at the Federal, State, County, or Municipal level must be found to be "Constitutional." The United States Supreme Court's "Justices," must from time to time rule on a given law's "constitutionality." Constitutionally speaking, the Supreme Court rules on legal issues brought before it. It also has the freedom to reverse itself. In 1856, the Court ruled that **AFRICAN** people could not even be deemed human beings (*Scott v. Sandford*). In 1896, it ruled that American society could be segregated (*Plessy v. Ferguson*). In 1954, it reversed

---

a force to be feared and reckoned with. Since the First World War, African preachers deemed to be radical subversives or threats to national security have been placed under surveillance and harassed by the Federal Government. The denomination they represented was irrelevant. Federal agents, *agent provocateurs*, and informants monitored Baptist and Pentecostals. Ironically, their views on America's participation in the Great War were irrelevant. Bishop C.H. Mason, organizer of the Church of God in Christ, condemned America's participation in "the War to Make the *World* Safe for Democracy," because Africans were not *safe* in America. Because of Bishop Mason's stand against the War, he was placed under observation. Robert M. Franklin, *Another Day's Journey: Black Churches Confront the American Crisis* (Minneapolis: Augsburg/Fortress Press, 1997), 50. Although the National Baptist Convention enthusiastically supported the War, its leadership was placed under surveillance. *The Commercial Appeal* (Memphis, TN), 31 March 1993.

effectively (*Brown v. the Board of Education*). It is worth noting that all Euro-American courts made the above rulings! With the power to reverse itself, it is conceivable that **AFRICAN** "Rights and Privileges" could be taken away. Does this sound impossible? During World War II, Japanese Americans living in the American West were rounded up and placed in concentration camps! The internment was never brought before the Court! These persons were loyal American citizens! It is quite plausible that one day, for whatever reason, African Federal law enforcement, Judges, high ranking military officers, and intelligence operatives could be spirited away to secret locations around the country and then used as human guinea pigs! Does this sound implausible? Remember the Tuskegee experiment was done under Federal aegis from the early 1930s to 1972! It could be done by configuring obscure Federal legislation, activated by a Presidential Executive Order, and upheld by the United States Supreme Court! The Federal military and law enforcement organs could then enforce it!

Another way of putting this would be to show with the self-perpetuating nature of the **United States Constitution** the government can do whatever it wants to **AFRICANS— *WHENEVER IT WANTS TO DO IT*!** All that needs to happen is for **AFRICANS** to be deemed "threats to the nation's security."

Format

The format I use throughout this book is simple. I present the relevant document with commentary. The commentary will point out, through a brief historical and social analysis of the words of the document, that **AFRICANS**, according to these assembled texts are considered to be less than nothing! I want to provide the reader with a historical and social *context* for understanding America's Sacred *Texts*!

I also edited the documents to substitute the word **AFRICAN** for **SLAVE**. In some cases, I placed the word **SLAVE** in upper case letters so as no to leave the reader with any doubts as to what the **AFRICAN'S** status was/is.

Thanks

Last, but certainly not least, I want to thank my wife Pat for her encouragement and support. I cannot mention the **AFRICAN** experience in America without extending to my long time friend, Rev. John Brinson, my deepest thanks for his critical review of my manuscript as well as points of discussion! Special thanks goes to Mrs. Tara Evans Bell and her editorial staff of The Juneteenth Publishing Group!

Pastor Michael S. Williams, D.Min.
Bayview Hunters Point
San Francisco, California
Juneteenth 2000

The Declaration of Independence (1776)

Perhaps one of the most fraudulent political, social, and economic upheavals in recent history was the so-called American "Revolution." The "Revolution," spanned the years 1770-1783. It began with a series of street riots in Boston (1770) and ended with the surrender of a sizable British army to a Virginia plantation/**SLAVE** owner by the name of George Washington in 1783, after the Battle of Yorktown (Virginia).

Popular mythology would have us believe that the "Revolution" was fought by heroic/selfless individuals sickened by the injustice of British rule over its North American colonies. The lofty words calling for "Freedom," were qualified by the notion of the colonials that persons of **AFRICAN** descent were to be tolerated as necessary evils at best or thought to be sub-human beings fit only for cotton, tobacco, and sugar cultivation.

The real reason for the Revolution was simple—**MONEY!** The colonies were Great Britain's **CASH COWS!** The Northern merchants and bankers, along with their Southern plantation owner cohorts, provided England with a plethora of goods and raw material! What really strained Great Britain's relationship with the colonies was its policy of **TAXATION**. The various **TAXATION** vehicles developed by the British Parliament deprived the British colonials of **CASH** that could, they felt and should have been, kept "Home." The tax legislation arising from the British Parliament during the 1760s and 1770s stoked the fires of "Revolution" against British "tyranny." The familiar colonial cry of "taxation without representation is tyranny" rings a bit hollow when looked at closely. The taxes levied against the colonials by the British parliament were done for the sake of paying for the large contingent of British troops needed to protect the colonials from French and Native American attacks. There was also the Spanish presence to be taken into consideration. The Spanish occupied territories such as Florida, which bordered Georgia and South Carolina, as well as vast tracts of land west of the Mississippi River. This meant that the British government was merely asking the colonials to assist in offsetting the cost of their *own* defense! By "doing the math," the colonials figured that they could displace the *British* colonial establishment with their *own*, tax their *own* people, provide for their *own* defense, produce their *own* goods, slaughter the Native American and enslave the **AFRICAN**—and most importantly, *not share the proceeds with anyone*!

The pathetic "foot soldiers," **AFRICAN** as well as Non-**AFRICAN,** were used as cannon fodder against Britain's well trained army. The leaders on the battlefield, as well as off, were primarily **MEN** of **MEANS,** i.e., **WHITE** bankers, professional **MEN,** and merchants in the North (such as John Hancock and John Adams). Many of these so-called "**FOUNDING FATHERS**" were political hacks, that, had there been no "Revolution," would have been forgotten, or would have had to face up to the fact that they were abject failures! In the South, the landed gentry, i.e., **SLAVE** holding plantation based aristocrats (such as *George Washington* and *Thomas Jefferson* the nation's *first* and *third* presidents, respectively) led the way.

By taking a close look at the colonial Declaration of Independence, one can see that far from being **FREEDOM'S CHARTER** for *ALL*, it was a thinly veiled attempt to provide a rational excuse for breaking away from Great Britain and at the same time for keeping **AFRICANS** in a less than human social position. The phrase, "All men are created equal," *did not* and *still does not* relate to the **AFRICAN**. The signatories of the Declaration of Independence, as well as the **US Constitution**, are often called the nation's **FOUNDING FATHERS**. They are the nation's *FATHERS*,[1] in the worst sense of the word. Their concept of **FATHER** gave them the excuse to rape, loot, and plunder the Western Hemisphere, massacre the Native American and **ENSLAVE** the **AFRICAN**. If anything, a viable alternative to the phrase "**FOUNDING FATHER**" could be "**FOUNDING FRAUD**." The Declaration of Independence, as well as the **US Constitution** were political instruments used to legitimize **AFRICAN ENSLAVEMENT** and the parasitic relationship

---

[1] The word "**FATHER**" derives from an Indo-European word for "**SENIOR MALE**." This word appears in several Indo-European language groups: *father* = English, *Vater* = German, *fader* = Gothic, *pater* = Latin, *pate'r* = Greek, *pita'r* = Sanskrit, *pedar* = Iranian. Curtis, *Indo-European Origins*, 12. The word "patriarch," derives from two Greek words, *pate'r* (father) and *archein* (to rule). The dynamics of patriarchy are alive and well in our time. Germans often call their country the "*Father*land." Persons that possess a high degree of "love" for their country are called "*patriot*s." The **President of the United States** was often portrayed, to Nineteenth Century Native Americans, as the "Great White *Father* in Washington." Until recently, members of city councils in American cities were called the "City *Fathers*." George Washington is often called the "*Father* of his country." The authors of the Declaration of Independence (1776), and the United States Constitution (1789), are often called America's **Founding *Fathers***.

between the British colonials and the American land mass. This parasitic relationship included a merciless as well as systematic slaughter of indigenous peoples whom had resided on this continent for nearly 12,000 years before the arrival of the first Europeans in 1492. Neither the Declaration nor the Constitution was formulated with any **AFRICAN** participation whatsoever. They referenced **AFRICANS** sometime directly, sometimes, indirectly.

The Declaration of Independence, as well as the **US Constitution** that mirrors it, is a **TERROR TEXT**.[15] They are the twin political nooses used to strangle the **AFRICAN**. They were meant to do so while the ink on their "**SACRED PAGES**" was drying. They continue to choke us!

Measures within the Declaration that relate to **ECONOMIC** complaints against the British Government, as well as to **AFRICANS** and **Native Americans** are highlighted. As you will see, this is no **FREEDOM** charter! It is a **TEXT of TERROR**.

---

[15] For a listing of the names, states represented, and occupations of the **FOUNDING FATHERS**, see **APPENDIX B**. In **APPENDIX B**, you will see which "FATHERS" signed the Declaration of Independence and which signed the Constitution. Some signed both!

The Declaration of Independence (1776)

The Signing of the Declaration of Independence
By the
Founding "Fathers" July 4, 1776

In Congress, July 4, 1776
The Unanimous Declaration of the Thirteen United States of America...

When in the Course of human events, it becomes necessary for one people to dissolve the political bands which have connected them with another, and to assume among the powers of the earth, the separate and equal station to which the Laws of Nature and of Nature's God entitle them, a decent respect to the opinions of mankind requires that they should declare the causes which impel them to the separation.

We hold these *truths to be self-evident, that all **men** are created equal*, that they are endowed by their Creator with certain unalienable Rights, that among these are Life, Liberty, and the pursuit of Happiness. --That to secure these rights, Governments are instituted among Men, deriving their just powers from the consent of the governed, --That whenever any Form of Government becomes destructive of these ends, it is the Right of the People to alter or to abolish it, and to institute new Government, laying its foundation on such principles and organizing its powers in such form, as to them shall seem most likely to effect their Safety and Happiness. Prudence, indeed, will dictate that Governments long established should not be changed for light and transient causes; and accordingly all experience hath shewn, that mankind are more disposed to suffer, while evils are sufferable, than to right themselves by abolishing the forms to which they are accustomed. But when a long train of abuses and usurpations, pursuing invariably the same Object evinces a design to reduce them under absolute Despotism, it is their right, it is their duty, to throw off such Government, and to provide new Guards for their future security.--Such has been the patient sufferance of these Colonies; and such is now the necessity which constrains them to alter their former Systems of Government. The history of the present King of Great Britain is a history of repeated injuries and usurpations, all having in direct object the establishment of an absolute Tyranny over these States. To prove this, let Facts be submitted to a candid world.

He has refused his Assent to Laws, the most wholesome and necessary for the public good.

He has forbidden his Governors to pass Laws of immediate and pressing importance, unless suspended in their operation till his Assent should be obtained; and when so suspended, he has utterly neglected to attend to them.

He has refused to pass other Laws for the accommodation of large districts of people, unless those people would relinquish the right of Representation in the Legislature, a right inestimable to them and formidable to tyrants only.

He has called together legislative bodies at places unusual, uncomfortable, and distant from the depository of their public Records, for the sole purpose of fatiguing them into compliance with his measures.

He has dissolved Representative Houses repeatedly, for opposing with manly firmness his invasions on the rights of the people.

He has refused for a long time, after such dissolutions, to cause others to be elected; whereby the Legislative powers, incapable of Annihilation, have returned to the People at large for their exercise; the State remaining in the mean time exposed to all the dangers of invasion from without, and convulsions within.

He has endeavored to prevent the population of these States; for that purpose obstructing the Laws for Naturalization of Foreigners; refusing to pass others to encourage their migrations hither, and raising the conditions of new Appropriations of Lands.

He has obstructed the Administration of Justice, by refusing his Assent to Laws for establishing Judiciary powers.

He has made Judges dependent on his Will alone, for the tenure of their offices, and the amount and payment of their salaries.

He has erected a multitude of New Offices, and sent hither swarms of Officers to harass our people, and eat out their substance.

He has kept among us, in times of peace, Standing Armies without the Consent of our legislatures.

He has affected to render the Military independent of and superior to the Civil power.

He has combined with others to subject us to a jurisdiction foreign to our constitution, and unacknowledged by our laws; giving his Assent to their Acts of pretended Legislation:

For Quartering large bodies of armed troops among us:

For protecting them, by a mock Trial, from punishment for any Murders which they should commit on the Inhabitants of these States:

For cutting off our Trade with all parts of the world:

For imposing Taxes on us without our Consent:

For depriving us in many cases, of the benefits of Trial by Jury:

For transporting us beyond Seas to be tried for pretended offences

For abolishing the free System of English Laws in a neighbouring Province, establishing therein an Arbitrary government, and enlarging its Boundaries so as to render it at once an example and fit instrument for introducing the same absolute rule into these Colonies:

For taking away our Charters, abolishing our most valuable Laws, and altering fundamentally the Forms of our Governments:

For suspending our own Legislatures, and declaring themselves invested with power to legislate for us in all cases whatsoever.

He has abdicated Government here, by declaring us out of his Protection and waging War against us.

He has plundered our seas, ravaged our Coasts, burnt our towns, and destroyed the lives of our people.

He is at this time transporting large Armies of foreign Mercenaries to compleat the works of death, desolation and tyranny, already begun with circumstances of Cruelty & perfidy scarcely paralleled in the most barbarous ages, and totally unworthy the Head of a civilized nation.

He has constrained our fellow Citizens taken Captive on the high Seas to bear Arms against their Country, to become the executioners of their friends and Brethren, or to fall themselves by their Hands.

He has excited domestic insurrections amongst us, and has endeavoured to bring on the inhabitants of our frontiers, the merciless Indian Savages, whose known rule of warfare, is an undistinguished destruction of all ages, sexes and conditions.

In every stage of these Oppressions We have Petitioned for Redress in the most humble terms: Our repeated Petitions have been answered only by repeated injury. A Prince whose character is thus marked by every act which may define a Tyrant, is unfit to be the ruler of a free people.

Nor have We been wanting in attentions to our British brethren. We have warned them from time to time of attempts by their legislature to extend an unwarrantable jurisdiction over us. We have reminded them of the circumstances of our emigration and settlement here. We have appealed to their native justice and magnanimity, and we have conjured them by the ties of our common kindred to disavow these usurpations, which, would inevitably interrupt our connections and correspondence. They too have been deaf to the voice of justice and of consanguinity. We must, therefore, acquiesce in the necessity, which denounces our Separation, and hold them, as we hold the rest of mankind, Enemies in War, in Peace Friends.

We, therefore, the Representatives of the united States of America, in General Congress, Assembled, appealing to the Supreme Judge of the world for the rectitude of our intentions, do, in the Name, and by Authority of the good People of these Colonies, solemnly publish and declare, That these United Colonies are, and of Right ought to be Free and Independent States; that they are Absolved from all Allegiance to the British Crown, and that all political connection between them and the State of Great Britain, is and ought to be totally dissolved; and that as Free and Independent States, they have full Power to levy War, conclude Peace, contract Alliances, establish Commerce, and to do all other Acts and Things which Independent States may of right do. And for the support of this Declaration, with a firm reliance on the protection of divine Providence, we mutually pledge to each other our Lives, our Fortunes and our sacred Honor.

**Thomas Jefferson
1743-1826
Native Virginian
Slave Holder
Author of the Declaration of Independence
Third President of the United States (1801-1809)**

Excerpts From Thomas Jefferson's *Notes on the State of Virginia* (1781-1782)

Perhaps one of the most ethically compromised "Founding Father" was Thomas Jefferson. Jefferson, a native Virginian, was a **SLAVEHOLDER**, man of letters, scientist, political theorist, and diplomat. He served as the "Revolutionary" Governor of Virginia and American Secretary of State during the Washington Administration. He also served as the nation's third President (1801-1809). Not only was he an official "Founding *FATHER*," but he also *FATHERED* several children by his **AFRICAN SLAVE**, Sally Hemmings. They were his *CHILDREN*—but they were also his *SLAVES*.

In the *Notes*, Jefferson reveals his deepest thoughts concerning the **AFRICAN'S** humanity, as well as his moral uneasiness concerning the institution of **SLAVERY**. He also acknowledged that God would one day punish America because of the practice of **SLAVERY**. Although Jefferson had qualms about **SLAVERY**, he never moved to abolish it during his lifetime.

I invite the reader to see for him/herself the deepest thoughts of the **Declaration of Independence's** human pen!

Excerpts From Thomas Jefferson's *Notes on the State of Virginia* (1781-1782)

THERE must doubtless be an unhappy influence on the manners of our people, produced by the existence of **SLAVERY** among us. The whole commerce between master and **SLAVE**, is a perpetual exercise of the most boisterous passions, the most unremitting despotism on the one part, and degrading submission on the other. Our children see this, and learn to imitate it; for man is an imitative animal. This quality is the germ of all education in him. From his cradle to his grave, he is learning to do what he sees others do. If a parent could find no motive either in his philanthropy or his self-love, for restraining the intemperance of passion towards his **SLAVE**, it should always be a sufficient one that his child is present. But generally, it is not sufficient. The parent storms, the child looks on, catches the lineaments of wrath, puts on the same airs in the circle of smaller **SLAVES**, gives a loose to his worst of passions, and thus nursed, educated, and daily exercised in tyranny, cannot but be stamped by it with odious peculiarities. The man must be a prodigy who can restrain his manners and morals, undepraved by such circumstances. And with what execration should the statesman be loaded, who, permitting one half the citizens thus to trample on the rights of the other, transforms those into despots, and these into enemies, destroys the morals of the one part, and the amor patriæ of the other. For if a **SLAVE** can have a country in this world, it must be any other in preference to that, in which he is born to live and labour for another: in which he must lock up the faculties of his nature, contribute, as far as depends on his individual endeavours, to the evanishment of the human race, or entail his own miserable condition on the endless generations proceeding from him. With the morals of the people, their industry also is destroyed. For in a warm climate, no man will labour for himself who can make another labour for him. This is so true, that of the proprietors of **SLAVES**, a very small portion indeed are ever seen to labour. *And can the liberties of a nation be thought secure, when we have removed their only firm basis, a conviction in the minds of the people that these liberties are of the gift of God? That they are not to be violated but with his wrath? Indeed I tremble for my country when I reflect that God is just: that his justice cannot sleep forever:* that considering NUMBERS, nature, and NATURAL MEANS only, a REVOLUTION of the wheel of fortune, an EXCHANGE of situations, is among possible events; that it may become possible by supernatural interference! The Almighty has no attribute which can take side with us in such a contest. -- But it is impossible to be temperate, and to pursue this subject through the various considerations of POLICY, of morals, of history, natural and civil. We must be contented to hope they will force their way into every one's mind. I think a CHANGE already perceptible, since the origin of the present revolution. The spirit of the master is abating, that of the **SLAVE** rising from the dust, his condition mollifying, the way, I hope preparing , under the AUSPICES of HEAVEN, for a TOTAL EMANCIPATION, and that this is disposed, in the order of events, to be with the consent of the masters, rather than by THEIR EXTIRPATION."

Mr. James Madison's Notes on the SLAVERY Debate at the Constitutional Convention (Tuesday, August 22, 1787)

James Madison, a **SLAVEHOLDING** delegate to the Constitutional Convention, from Virginia took the following notes. They related to the debates at the Convention surrounding the issue of **SLAVERY**. The notes betray an obvious flaw in America's Constitutional process. The debate was undertaken by Whites. The debate focused on the position of **SLAVES** in the new nation. It was also conducted with no **AFRICAN** input!

Madison would also go on to serve as the fourth **President of the United States** (1809-1817). During the Constitutional debate, he never discloses his own views on the subject of **SLAVERY**. However, in **Appendix A**, we see his undiluted views of **AFRICAN SLAVES**.

Mr. James Madison's Notes on the SLAVERY Debate at the Constitutional Convention (Tuesday, August 22, 1787)

IN CONVENTION

Art VII sect 4. resumed. **Mr. SHERMAN** was for leaving the clause as it stands. He disapproved of the **SLAVE** trade; yet as the States were now possessed of the right to import **SLAVES**, as the public good did not require it to be taken from them, & as it was expedient to have as few objections as possible to the proposed scheme of Government, he thought it best to leave the matter as we find it. He observed that the abolition of **SLAVERY** seemed to be going on in the U. S. & that the good sense of the several States would probably by degrees complete it. He urged on the Convention the necessity of dispatching its business.

Colonel MASON. This infernal traffic originated in the avarice of British Merchants. The British Govt. constantly checked the attempts of Virginia to put a stop to it. The present question concerns not the importing States alone but the whole Union. The evil of having **SLAVES** was experienced during the late war. Had **SLAVES** been treated as they might have been by the Enemy, they would have proved dangerous instruments in their hands. But their folly dealt by the **SLAVES**, as it did by the Tories. He mentioned the dangerous insurrections of the **SLAVES** in Greece and Sicily; and the instructions given by Cromwell to the **COMMISSIONERS** sent to Virginia, to arm the servants & **SLAVES**, in case other means of obtaining its submission should fail. Maryland & Virginia he said had already prohibited the importation of **SLAVES** expressly. N. Carolina had done the same in substance. All this would be in vain if S. Carolina & Georgia be at liberty to import. The Western people are already calling out for **SLAVES** for their new lands, and will fill that Country with **SLAVES** if they can be got thro' S. Carolina & Georgia. **SLAVERY** discourages arts & manufactures. The poor despise labor when performed by **SLAVES**. They prevent the immigration of Whites, who really enrich & strengthen a Country. They produce the most pernicious effect on manners. Every master of **SLAVES** is born a petty tyrant. They bring the judgment of heaven on a Country. As nations can not be rewarded or punished in the next world they must be in this. By an inevitable chain of causes & effects providence punishes national sins, by national calamities. He lamented that some of our Eastern brethren had from a lust of gain embarked in this nefarious traffic. As to the States being in possession of the Right to import, this was the case with many other rights, now to be properly given up. He held it essential in every point of view that the Genl. Govt. should have power to prevent the increase of **SLAVERY**.

Mr. ELSWORTH. As he had never owned a **SLAVE** could not judge of the effects of **SLAVERY** on character: He said however that if it was to be considered in a moral light we ought to go farther and free those already in the Country. -As **SLAVES** also multiply so fast in Virginia & & Maryland that it is cheaper to raise than import them, whilst in the sickly rice swamps foreign supplies are necessary, if we go no farther than is urged, we shall be unjust towards S. Carolina & Georgia. Let us not intermeddle. As population increases poor laborers will be so plenty as to render **SLAVES** useless. **SLAVERY** in time will not be a speck in our Country. Provision is already made in Connecticut for abolishing it. And the abolition has already taken place in Massachusetts. As to the danger of insurrections from foreign influence, that will become a motive to kind treatment of the **SLAVES**.

Mr. PINKNEY. If **SLAVERY** be wrong, it is justified by the example of all the world. He cited the case of Greece Rome & other ancient States; the sanction given by France England, Holland & other modern States. In all ages one half of mankind have been **SLAVES**. If the S. States were let alone they will probably of themselves stop importations. He wd. himself as a Citizen of S. Carolina vote for it. An attempt to take away the right as proposed will produce serious objections to the Constitution which he wished to see adopted.

GENERAL PINKNEY declared it to be his firm opinion that if himself & all his colleagues were to sign the Constitution & use their personal influence, it would be of no avail towards obtaining the assent of their Constituents. S. Carolina & Georgia cannot do without **SLAVES**. As to Virginia she will gain by stopping the importations. Her **SLAVES** will rise in value, & she has more than she wants. It would be unequal to require S. C. & Georgia to confederate on such unequal terms. He said the Royal assent before the Revolution had never been refused to S. Carolina as to Virginia. He contended that the importation of **SLAVES** would be for the interest of the whole Union. The more **SLAVES**, the more produce to employ the carrying trade;

The more consumption also, and the more of this, the more of revenue for the common treasury. He admitted it to be reasonable that **SLAVES** should be dutied like other imports, but should consider a rejection of the clause as an exclusion of S. Carolina. from the Union.

Mr. BALDWIN had conceived national objects alone to be before the Convention, not such as like the present were of a local nature. Georgia was decided on this point. That State has always hitherto supposed a Genl. Government. to be the pursuit of the central States who wished to have a vortex for every thing- that her distance would preclude her from equal advantage-& that she could not prudently purchase it by yielding national powers. From this it might be understood in what light she would view an attempt to abridge one of her favorite prerogatives. If left to herself, she may probably put a stop to the evil. As one ground for this conjecture, he took notice of the sect of -------- which he said was a respectable class of people, who carried their ethics beyond the mere equality of men, extending their humanity to the claims of the whole animal creation.

Mr. WILSON observed that if S. C. & Georgia were themselves disposed to get rid of the importation of **SLAVES** in a short time as had been suggested, they would never refuse to Unite because the importation might be prohibited. As the Section now stands all articles imported are to be taxed. **SLAVES** alone are exempt. This is in fact a bounty on that article.

Mr. GERRY thought we had nothing to do with the conduct of the States as to **SLAVES**, but ought to be careful not to give any sanction to it.

Mr. DICKENSON considered it as inadmissible on every principle of honor & safety that the importation of **SLAVES** should be authorized to the States by the Constitution. The true question was whether the national happiness would be promoted or impeded by the importation, and this question ought to be left to the National Govt. not to the States particularly interested. If Engd. & France permit **SLAVERY**, **SLAVES** are at the same time excluded from both those Kingdoms. Greece and Rome were made unhappy by their **SLAVES**. He could not believe that the Southn. States would refuse to confederate on the account apprehended; especially as the power was not likely to be immediately exercised by the Genl. Government.

Mr. WILLIAMSON stated the law of N. Carolina on the subject, to wit that it did not directly prohibit the importation of **SLAVES**. It imposed a duty of 5. on each **SLAVE** imported from **AFRICA**. 10 on each from elsewhere, & 50 on each from a State licensing manumission. He thought the S. States could not be members of the Union if the clause shd. be rejected, and that it was wrong to force any thing down, not absolutely necessary, and which any State must disagree to.

Mr. KING thought the subject should be considered in a political light only. If two States will not agree to the Constitution as stated on one side, he could affirm with equal belief on the other, that great & equal opposition would be experienced from the other States. He remarked on the exemption of **SLAVES** from duty whilst every other import was subjected to it, as an inequality that could not fail to strike the commercial sagacity of the Northn. & middle States.

Mr. LANGDON was strenuous for giving the power to the Genl. Govt. He cd. not with a good conscience leave it with the States who could then go on with the traffic, without being restrained by the opinions here given that they will themselves cease to import **SLAVES**.

Genl. **PINKNEY** thought himself bound to declare candidly that he did not think S. Carolina would stop her importations of **SLAVES** in any short time, but only stop them occasionally as she now does. He moved to commit the clause that **SLAVES** might be made liable to an equal tax with other imports which he thought right & wch. wd. remove one difficulty that had been started.

Mr. RUTLIDGE. If the Convention thinks that N. C. S. C. & Georgia will ever agree to the plan, unless their right to import **SLAVES** be untouched, the expectation is vain. The people of those States will never be such fools as to give up so important an interest. He was strenuous agst. striking out the Section, and seconded the motion of Genl. Pinkney for a commitment.

Mr. Govr. MORRIS wished the whole subject to be committed including the clauses relating to taxes on exports & to a navigation act. These things may form a bargain among the Northern & Southern States.

Mr. BUTLER declared that he never would agree to the power of taxing exports.

Mr. SHERMAN said it was better to let the S. States import **SLAVES** than to part with them, if they made that a sine qua non. He was opposed to a tax on **SLAVES** imported as making the matter worse, because it implied they were property. He acknowledged that if the power of prohibiting the importation should be given to the Genl. Government that it would be exercised. He thought it would be its duty to exercise the power.

Mr. READ was for the commitment provided the clause concerning taxes on exports should also be committed.

Mr. SHERMAN observed that that clause had been agreed to & therefore could not committed.

Mr. RANDOLPH was for committing in order that some middle ground might, if possible, be found. He could never agree to the clause as it stands. He wd. sooner risk the constitution. He dwelt on the dilemma to which the Convention was exposed. By agreeing to the clause, it would revolt the Quakers, the Methodists, and many others in the States having no **SLAVES**. On the other hand, two States might be lost to the Union. Let us then, he said, try the chance of a commitment.

Excerpts From The United States Constitution (1787)

The Delegates to the Constitutional Convention

The **Constitution of the United States of America** was submitted to the so-called "Continental Congress" on September 17, 1787.[1] It was ratified by the requisite

---

[1] The ratification process, which arose out of the Constitutional Convention, is as follows. Below, not only will you see the process but you also need to read the to read the names of the signatories! Finally, I provided a list of states that ratified the Constitution. By their assent to the ratification process, they explicitly agreed that Africans were to be considered for all practical purposes, non-human commodities! Read it for yourself!

Article V. - Amendment

The Congress, whenever two thirds of both Houses shall deem it necessary, shall propose Amendments to this Constitution, or, on the Application of the Legislatures of two thirds of the several States, shall call a Convention for proposing Amendments, which, in either Case, shall be valid to all Intents and Purposes, as part of this Constitution, when ratified by the Legislatures of three fourths of the several States, or by Conventions in three fourths thereof, as the one or the other Mode of Ratification may be proposed by the Congress; Provided that no Amendment which may be made prior to the Year One thousand eight hundred and eight shall in any Manner affect the first and fourth Clauses in the Ninth Section of the first Article; and that no State, without its Consent, shall be deprived of its equal Suffrage in the Senate.

Article VII. - Ratification

The Ratification of the Conventions of nine States, shall be sufficient for the Establishment of this Constitution between the States so ratifying the same.

Done in Convention by the Unanimous Consent of the States present the Seventeenth Day of September in the Year of our Lord one thousand seven hundred and Eighty seven and of the Independence of the United States of America the Twelfth. In Witness whereof We have hereunto subscribed our Names.
George Washington - **President** and deputy from *Virginia*

number of states by mid-1788 (nine states were needed). This gave this document the force of law. The **Constitution of the United States** distills, in written form, the power(s) of the Federal Government. But it also put into force the musings and comments of the persons in the previous section concerning their views of **AFRICANS**. This is well known. What is *not* so well known is that it also chiseled in (legal) stone who *was* "human" and who *was not*. To put it bluntly, the discussions we reviewed in the last section on the status of **AFRICAN SLAVES** are now given the force of law. **ENSLAVED**

New Hampshire - **John Langdon, Nicholas Gilman**
Massachusetts - **Nathaniel Gorham, Rufus King**
Connecticut - **Wm Saml Johnson, Roger Sherman**
New York - **Alexander Hamilton**
New Jersey - **Wil Livingston, David Brearley, Wm Paterson, Jona. Dayton**
Pennsylvania - **B Franklin, Thomas Mifflin, Robt Morris, Geo. Clymer, Thos FitzSimons, Jared Ingersoll, James Wilson, Gouv Morris**
Delaware - **Geo. Read, Gunning Bedford jun, John Dickinson, Richard Bassett, Jaco. Broom**
Maryland - **James McHenry, Dan of St Tho Jenifer, Danl Carroll**
Virginia - **John Blair, James Madison Jr.**
North Carolina - **Wm Blount, Richd Dobbs Spaight, Hu Williamson**
South Carolina - **J. Rutledge, Charles Cotesworth Pinckney, Charles Pinckney, Pierce Butler**
Georgia - **William Few, Abr Baldwin**
Attest: **William Jackson**, Secretary

The following states ratified the Constitution in the following order:

Delaware September 12, 1787, **Pennsylvania** December 12, 1787, **New Jersey** December 18, 1787, **Connecticut** January 9, 1788, **Georgia** February 2, 1788, Massachusetts February 6, 1788, **Maryland** April 28, 1788, **South Carolina** May 23, 1788, **New Hampshire** June 21, 1788 , - *Constitution Ratified* **1788.**

AFRICANS were classified as being **3/5**[th] of a human being! [2] This meant that they were considered by the **SLAVE** holding Constitutional signatories as well as the non-**SLAVE** holding signatories as being less than human! The **AFRICAN'S** less than human status was then given **LEGAL SANCTION**. Legal (*de jure*) as well as **CUSTOMARY** (*de facto*) views on the status of the **AFRICAN** would, with the ratification process, then be *the* point of reference concerning the **AFRICAN'S** place in American Society—it was true *then*, and it is certainly true *now!*

Below, you will find excerpts from the Constitution. These excerpts relate to the three "Branches" of the Federal Government. They are as follows: The Congress, Executive, and the Judiciary. Each has, historically, played its part in making sure that persons of **AFRICAN** descent were **ENSLAVED**, kept under surveillance, lynched, experimented upon, or a combination of all of the above!

I've isolated the three branches of government, the Legislative, Executive, and Judicial. The three tentacles of the Federal Government, as well as their counterparts at the State, County,

---

[2] The Southern States *insisted* upon this clause! This clause was the **PRICE OF FEDERAL UNION**! The inclusion of this clause proves beyond a shadow of a doubt that the "Founding *Fathers*" should really be called the "Founding *Frauds!*" The Southern delegates devised this cynical formula as a way of boosting their population numbers. This was needed so as not to allow the more populous Northern States from overwhelming them in the lower chamber of the Congress, the House of Representatives! "House" seats are distributed according to census/population figures. The formula is laid out in **Article I, Section 2, Clause 3**.

and local levels, were designed to work in unison, or at least not at cross purposes! The Federal Government, via the **US Constitution**, reigns supreme over the lesser governments. Federal jurisdiction outstrips the lessor forms of government. For example, the President has ultimate jurisdiction over all other executive leaders, i.e., state governors, county administrators, and mayors. The **President of the United States** is the administrator of the Executive branch of government. Under his authority are the Executive "departments," headed by "secretaries," (i.e., the "Secretary" of ...State, War/Defense, Agriculture, etc. The nation's chief "law" *enforcer's* title is the "Attorney General"). The Federal Congress can overrule *any*, and I mean *any, law passed* by a state legislature, County Board of Supervisors (in some states they are called County Commissioners) or City Council. The **US Supreme Court** has the **FINAL** say over rulings coming from the Federal Courts of Appeal, and Federal District Courts, State Supreme Courts, and County Courts.

Each branch of the Federal Government has played its **LEGAL/CONSTITUIONAL** role in the oppression of **AFRICAN** people. Its role is **CONSTITUIONAL**, therefore **LEGAL**! I do believe I hear some **AFRICANS** that feel as if they have "made it within the system" protesting! They take pride in their role as back stabbing opportunists! What they have done to their own people, on behalf of "Massa" would shame Brutus, Julius Caesar's "friend/assassin," Judas, a paid informant that betrayed Jesus, Benedict Arnold, George Washington's "friend" and "Revolutionary War" Hero who surrendered West Point to the British! At worst, they would bring down upon their heads the worst condemnation of even the so-called "Kapos." The "Kapos" were Jews that served the Nazis in the Death Camps. They led their fellow Jews to the slaughter, while believing that they would be spared the oven! While the Kapos suffered the delusion that their participation in the genocide of their co-religionists would spare them from the hideous tortures of the Nazi extermination machine, one can only imagine the surprise when they, *too*, were ushered into the ovens by their Nazi "friends!" Such deluded "House **SLAVES**" are only a hair's breath away from professional, social, physical, and financial annihilation!

There is not enough space to chronicle the crimes of the Federal Government against **AFRICAN** people! Recent examples should suffice! The United States Department of Justice's **Federal Bureau of Investigation**, an arm of the Executive Branch of government, has a history of violating **AFRICAN** personhood.[3] From 1932-1972, the US Department of Public Health, an offshoot of the Executive Branch of government, "studied" the effects of syphilis upon **AFRICAN** men, without their consent. Had it not been exposed in 1972, it would have continued. In fact, it probably is still continuing—maybe under the guise of AIDS.[4] There is strong evidence that the **Central**

---

[3] Kenneth O'Reilly, *Black Americans and the FBI Files*, (New York: Carroll & Graf) 1994.

[4] James H. Jones, *Bad Blood: The Tuskegee Syphilis Experiment* (New York: The Free Press, 1993), ix-x, 1. This revelation has caused many observers to believe that the AIDS virus was developed by the government to eradicate African peoples, Ibid. Also, Haki R. Madhubuti, *Black Men Obsolete, Single, Dangerous?:*

Intelligence Agency, another offshoot of the Executive branch of the Federal Government facilitated the importation of Cocaine into the **AFRICAN** community, stranger still, but not improbable, that same agency may have played a hand in the massacre of nearly 900 **AFRICANS** at Jonestown, back in the late 1970s.[5]

All of the above stated "High Crimes and Misdemeanors" are constitutionally sanctioned activities by the **United States Government**. All of the above-named crimes, perpetrated against **AFRICAN** peoples, were/are done so with the feeble acquiescence of the **Legislative** and **Judicial** branches of government! Congress funds these criminal activities. Not only does it fund the activities, but it passes the necessary legislation giving the Executive Branch of Government the "legal" mandate in which to crucify persons of **AFRICAN** descent, even to this day! The **Judiciary** then "interprets" the Constitution in such a

---

Afrikan-American Families in Transition: Essays in Discovery, Solution and Hope (Chicago: Third World Press, 1991), 51-57.

[5] Michael Meiers, *Was Jonestown a CIA Medical Experiment? : A Review of the Evidence* (Lewiston, NY: The Edwin Mellen Press, 1988). The Central Intelligence Agency, has had its hand in the international drug trade. It has done so with a devastating impact upon the African community in America. Alfred W. McCoy *The Politics of Heroin: CIA Complicity In the Global Drug Trade.* (Brooklyn, NY: Lawrence Hill Books, 1991). Gary. Webb, *Dark Alliance: The CIA, the Contras, and the Crack Cocaine Explosion* (New York: Seven Stories Press, 1998). John Jacob Nutter, Ph.D. *The CIA's Black Ops: Covert Action, Foreign Policy, and Democracy* (Amherst, NY: Prometheus Books, 2000). All of the nefarious activities listed above were/are perpetrated against the African community with the "legality" of the **US Constitution** as a shield!

way as to ensure the self-perpetuating "Constitutional" monstrosity known as **AMERICA**. In fact, the corrupt seeds planted by the so-called "**FOUNDING FATHERS**" have produced particularly bitter fruit of late! In 1978, the Congress passed the Foreign Intelligence Surveillance Act (**FISA**). President Jimmy Carter signed it into law, and its constitutionality has never been challenged successfully in a court of "law." The **FISA**, augmented by President Bill Clinton's **Executive Order Number 12949**, tears away the façades and fraud of Constitutional "protection." The **FISA** gives the three branches of the Federal Government the unprecedented power to circumvent Civil "liberties" and to do whatever they want to do in the name of *National Security*! [6] President Clinton's Executive Order, combined with the **FISA**,

---

[6] For the full reading of this "text of terror," I would encourage you to order a copy of it from your congressperson, or access it on the World Wide Web. In summary, it allows the following to occur: The **FISA** provides for a seven-man court, made up of Federal District Court judges. The Chief Justice of the Supreme Court appoints these judges. This court meets in secret, with no public accountability. If federal prosecutors believe that you are worthy of investigation, then you *will* be targeted. Any law enforcement agency, within the Federal Government, can then make you their "project." It makes no difference, it can be the **FBI**, **CIA**, **DEA**, the alphabet configuration is irrelevant. Your property can be searched with or without your knowledge, with or without a warrant. They need never reveal their motives to you, in whole or in part! All of these activities are done in the name of "protecting" our way of "life," or in the interest of "national (in) security. With such power at their disposal, even **AFRICANS** that, erroneously believe, that they have "made it" within the system (by attaining the rank of Special Agents, Investigators, prosecutors, Judges, etc., especially at the Federal level) need to be careful! The same people they think are their "friends" will turn on them and break them! It will be "legal" too! "**House NEGROES**" that have outlived their usefulness can, and most certainly *will be* "taken care of!" *NOTE*: A full text of President Clinton's **Executive Order #12949** can be found on **Page 215 (APPENDIX G)**.

effectively tears away the façade of the Constitution's precedence over the activities of government. With the **FISA**, the United States Government has formally detached itself from the Constitution and has become a law unto itself. It can do anything it wants to do—*because it can!*

Keep all of this in mind as you read the excerpts from the **US Constitution**! If there was ever a document that could literally be called a "**TEXT of TERROR**," this is the one! If such draconian laws were drafted by another country, America would then sit on its high horse and list that country as a facilitator of **STATE SPONSORED TERRORISM.**

PORTIONS OF THE UNITED STATES CONSTITUION

We the People of the United States, in Order to form a more perfect Union, establish Justice, insure domestic Tranquility, provide for the common defence, promote the general Welfare, and secure the Blessings of Liberty to ourselves and our Posterity, do ordain and establish this Constitution for the United States of America.

Article. I.
Section 1.
All legislative Powers herein granted shall be vested in a Congress of the United States, which shall consist of a Senate and House of Representatives.
Section. 2.
Clause 1: The House of Representatives shall be composed of Members chosen every second Year by the People of the several States, and the Electors in each State shall have the Qualifications requisite for Electors of the most numerous Branch of the State Legislature.
Clause 2: No Person shall be a Representative who shall not have attained to the Age of twenty five Years, and been seven Years a Citizen of the United States, and who shall not, when elected, be an Inhabitant of that State in which he shall be chosen.
Clause 3: *Representatives and direct Taxes shall be* **apportioned** *among the several States which may be included within this Union, according to their respective* **Numbers**, *which*

shall be determined by adding to the whole Number of free Persons, including those bound to Service for a Term of Years, and excluding Indians not taxed, **THREE FIFTHS OF ALL OTHER**.[3]

Article. II.
Section. 1.
Clause 1: The executive Power shall be vested in a **President of the United States** of America. He shall hold his Office during the Term of four Years, and, together with the Vice President, chosen for the same Term, be elected, as follows

Clause 2: Each State shall appoint, in such Manner as the Legislature thereof may direct, a Number of Electors, equal to the whole Number of Senators and Representatives to which the State may be entitled in the Congress: but no Senator or Representative, or Person holding an Office of Trust or Profit under the United States, shall be appointed an Elector.

Clause 3: The Electors shall meet in their respective States, and vote by Ballot for two Persons, of whom one at least shall not be an Inhabitant of the same State with themselves. And they shall make a List of all the Persons voted for, and of the Number of Votes for each; which List they shall sign and certify, and transmit sealed to the Seat of the Government of the United

---

[3] "Free" Persons = Whites and "Free" Blacks, "Bound to Service for a number of years = indentured servants. An indentured servant is a person that obligates him/herself to "serve" another for a specified number of years. Indians, that were not considered to be "tax payers" were excluded from the population count (This is ironic—the Native American's residency in "America" began at least 9,000-10,000 years prior to the arrival of the White man!). $3/5^{th}$ *of all "others," refers to enslaved Africans.*

States, directed to the President of the Senate. The President of the Senate shall, in the Presence of the Senate and House of Representatives, open all the Certificates, and the Votes shall then be counted. The Person having the greatest Number of Votes shall be the President, if such Number be a Majority of the whole Number of Electors appointed; and if there be more than one who have such Majority, and have an equal Number of Votes, then the House of Representatives shall immediately chuse by Ballot one of them for President; and if no Person have a Majority, then from the five highest on the List the said House shall in like Manner chuse the President. But in chusing the President, the Votes shall be taken by States, the Representation from each State having one Vote; A quorum for this Purpose shall consist of a Member or Members from two thirds of the States, and a Majority of all the States shall be necessary to a Choice. In every Case, after the Choice of the President, the Person having the greatest Number of Votes of the Electors shall be the Vice President. But if there should remain two or more who have equal Votes, the Senate shall chuse from them by Ballot the Vice President. *(See Note 8)*

Clause 4: The Congress may determine the Time of chusing the Electors, and the Day on which they shall give their Votes; which Day shall be the same throughout the United States.

Clause 5: No Person except a natural born Citizen, or a Citizen of the United States, at the time of the Adoption of this Constitution, shall be eligible to the Office of President; neither shall any Person be eligible to that Office who shall not have attained to the Age of thirty five Years, and been fourteen Years a Resident within the United States.

Clause 6: In Case of the Removal of the President from Office, or of his Death, Resignation, or Inability to discharge the Powers and Duties of the said Office, *(See Note 9)* the Same shall devolve on the Vice President, and the Congress may by Law provide for the Case of Removal, Death, Resignation or Inability, both of the President and Vice President, declaring what Officer shall then act as President, and such Officer shall act accordingly, until the Disability be removed, or a President shall be elected.

Clause 7: The President shall, at stated Times, receive for his Services, a Compensation, which shall neither be encreased nor diminished during the Period for which he shall have been elected, and he shall not receive within that Period any other Emolument from the United States, or any of them.

Clause 8: Before he enter on the Execution of his Office, he shall take the following Oath or Affirmation:--"I do solemnly swear (or affirm) that I will faithfully execute the Office of **President of the United States**, and will to the best of my Ability, preserve, protect and defend the Constitution of the United States."

Section. 2.

Clause 1: The President shall be Commander in Chief of the Army and Navy of the United States, and of the Militia of the several States, when called into the actual Service of the United States; he may require the Opinion, in writing, of the principal Officer in each of the executive Departments, upon any Subject relating to the Duties of their respective Offices, and he shall have Power to grant Reprieves and Pardons for Offences against the United States, except in Cases of Impeachment.

Clause 2: He shall have Power, by and with the Advice and Consent of the Senate, to make Treaties, provided two thirds of the Senators present concur; and he shall nominate, and by and with the Advice and Consent of the Senate, shall appoint Ambassadors, other public Ministers and Consuls, Judges of the supreme Court, and all other Officers of the United States, whose Appointments are not herein otherwise provided for, and which shall be established by Law: but the Congress may by Law vest the Appointment of such inferior Officers, as they think proper, in the President alone, in the Courts of Law, or in the Heads of Departments.

Clause 3: The President shall have Power to fill up all Vacancies that may happen during the Recess of the Senate, by granting Commissions which shall expire at the End of their next Session.

Section. 3.

He shall from time to time give to the Congress Information of the State of the Union, and recommend to their Consideration such Measures as he shall judge necessary and expedient; he may, on extraordinary Occasions, convene both Houses, or either of them, and in Case of Disagreement between them, with Respect to the Time of Adjournment, he may adjourn them to such Time as he shall think proper; he shall receive Ambassadors and other public Ministers; he shall take Care that the Laws be faithfully executed, and shall Commission all the Officers of the United States.

Section. 4.

The President, Vice President and all civil Officers of the United States, shall be removed from Office on Impeachment for, and

Conviction of, Treason, Bribery, or other high Crimes and Misdemeanors.

Article III.
Section. 1.

The judicial Power of the United States, shall be vested in one supreme Court, and in such inferior Courts as the Congress may from time to time ordain and establish. The Judges, both of the supreme and inferior Courts, shall hold their Offices during good Behaviour, and shall, at stated Times, receive for their Services, a Compensation, which shall not be diminished during their Continuance in Office.

Section. 2.
Clause 1:

The judicial Power shall extend to all Cases, in Law and Equity, arising under this Constitution, the Laws of the United States, and Treaties made, or which shall be made, under their Authority; --to all Cases affecting Ambassadors, other public Ministers and Consuls; --to all Cases of admiralty and maritime Jurisdiction; --to Controversies to which the United States shall be a Party; --to Controversies between two or more States; --*between a State and Citizens of another State;* between Citizens of different States,--between Citizens of the same State claiming Lands under Grants of different States, and *between a State, or the Citizens thereof, and foreign States, Citizens or Subjects.*

Clause 2:

In all Cases affecting Ambassadors, other public Ministers and Consuls, and those in which a State shall be Party, the Supreme Court shall have original Jurisdiction. In all the other Cases before mentioned, the Supreme Court shall have appellate Jurisdiction, both as to Law and Fact, with such Exceptions, and under such Regulations as the Congress shall make.

Clause 3:

The Trial of all Crimes, except in Cases of Impeachment, shall be by Jury; and such Trial shall be held in the State where the said Crimes shall have been committed; but when not committed within any State, the Trial shall be at such Place or Places as the Congress may by Law have directed.

The Fugitive Slave Act of 1850

The **Fugitive Slave Act of 1850**, was not the first such "Act" of Congress,[1] but it was perhaps the most infamous. As you read this document, be aware that it was **passed** by the **United States Congress**, and **signed into law** by the nation's **thirteenth President, Millard Fillmore, in September of 1850**. Perhaps the most interesting thing about this "Act," was that it created a classification of *FEDERAL AGENTS*[2] known as **COMMISSIONERS**. These **COMMISSIONERS** were to preside over the retrieval of escaped **SLAVES**. The duties of these **FEDERAL AGENTS** are spelled out in detail throughout the Act's text. Read it for yourself!

The **Fugitive Slave Act of 1850**, effectively gave *all* **AFRICANS** in both the South and the North, the status of **SLAVES**. Why? Because it allowed bounty hunters, aided and abetted by **Federal** courts and law enforcement officials, to "capture" and return runaway **SLAVES**. The burden of proof to "prove" their "free" status was then laid upon the "free"

---

[1] The first Fugitive **SLAVE** Act was passed by the Congress in 1793 and signed into law by the "Father" of his country, and first president, Virginia born **SLAVE** owner—George Washington.

[2] Federal Agents are the enforcement arms of the Federal Government. The may wear the title of Special Agent, Marshal, etc., the exact name and title is irrelevant. Their function is to dispassionately "enforce" the "laws" of the United States Government. Their authority derives from laws passed by the Congress. The President then signs the law. Unless the Supreme Court rules that the law violates the letter/spirit of the **US Constitution**, the law will be enforced! The law may not be moral or even ethical, but it is legal!

AFRICANS. If they could not prove their "free" status, they would then become the property of a **SLAVE** owner. Barring an escape, facilitated by sympathetic Quakers or the Underground Railroad, the captured **SLAVES** or **ENSLAVED** "free" **AFRICANS** were doomed to **SLAVERY** until the day they died, escaped, or if they lived long enough, until the end of the Civil War.

The Fugitive **SLAVE** Act's "Constitutionality" was never challenged in the nation's court system.

The Fugitive Slave Act of 1850

Section 1

Be it enacted by the Senate and House of Representatives of the United States of America in Congress assembled, That the persons who have been, or may hereafter be, appointed **COMMISSIONERS**,[1] in virtue of any act of Congress, by the Circuit Courts of the United States, and Who, in consequence of such appointment, are authorized to exercise the powers that any justice of the peace, or other magistrate of any of the United States, may exercise in respect to offenders for any crime or offense against the United States, *by arresting, imprisoning, or bailing* the same under and by the virtue of the thirty-third section of the act of the twenty-fourth of September seventeen hundred and eighty-nine, entitled "An Act to establish the judicial courts of the United States" shall be,[2] and are

---

[1] These **COMMISSIONERS**, while not judges, were empowered to implement the provisions of the Fugitive **SLAVE** Act. This office was specifically created to deal with **AFRICANS** in a way that the courts could not. Read on!

[2] This section of the "Act" references the following in the **US Constitution**:

Article III.
Section. 1.
The judicial Power of the United States, shall be vested in one supreme Court, and in such inferior Courts as the Congress may from time to time ordain and establish. The Judges, both of the supreme and inferior Courts, shall hold their Offices during good Behaviour, and shall, at stated Times, receive for their Services, a Compensation, which shall not be diminished during their Continuance in Office.

hereby, authorized and required to exercise and discharge all the powers and duties conferred by this act.

Section 2

And be it further enacted, That the Superior Court of each organized Territory of the United States shall have the same power to appoint **COMMISSIONERS** to take acknowledgments of bail and affidavits, and to take depositions of witnesses in civil causes, which is now possessed by the Circuit Court of the United States; and all **COMMISSIONERS** who shall hereafter be appointed for such purposes by the Superior Court of any organized Territory of the United States, shall possess all the powers, and exercise all the duties, conferred by law upon the **COMMISSIONERS** appointed by the Circuit Courts of the United States for similar purposes, and shall moreover exercise and discharge all the powers and duties conferred by this act.

Section. 2.

Clause 1:

The judicial Power shall extend to all Cases, in Law and Equity, arising under this Constitution, the Laws of the United States, and Treaties made, or which shall be made, under their Authority; --to all Cases affecting Ambassadors, other public Ministers and Consuls; --to all Cases of admiralty and maritime Jurisdiction; --to Controversies to which the United States shall be a Party; --to Controversies between two or more States; --*between a State and Citizens of another State;* between Citizens of different States,--between Citizens of the same State claiming Lands under Grants of different States, and *between a State, or the Citizens thereof, and foreign States, Citizens or Subjects.*

Section 3

And be it further enacted, That the Circuit Courts of the United States shall from time to time enlarge the number of the **COMMISSIONERS**, with a view to afford reasonable facilities to reclaim fugitives from labor [**ESCAPED SLAVES**], and to the prompt discharge of the duties imposed by this act.

Section 4

And be it further enacted, That the **COMMISSIONERS** above named shall have concurrent jurisdiction with the judges of the Circuit and District Courts of the United States, in their respective circuits and districts within the several States, and the judges of the Superior Courts of the Territories, severally and collectively, in term-time and vacation; shall grant certificates to such claimants, upon satisfactory proof being made, with authority to take and remove such fugitives from service or labor, under the restrictions herein contained, to the State or Territory from which such [**AFRICAN SLAVES**] may have escaped or fled.

Section 5

And be it further enacted, That it shall be the duty of all marshals and deputy marshals[3] to obey and execute all warrants and precepts issued under the provisions of this act, when to them directed; and should any marshal or deputy marshal refuse to receive such warrant, or other process, when tendered, or to use all proper means diligently to execute the same, he shall, on conviction thereof, be fined in the sum of one thousand dollars, to the use of such claimant, on the motion of such claimant, by the Circuit or District Court for the district of such marshal; and after arrest of such fugitive, by such marshal or his deputy, or whilst at any time in his custody under the provisions of this act, should such fugitive escape, whether with or without the assent of such marshal or his deputy, such marshal shall be liable, on his official bond, to be prosecuted for the benefit of such claimant, for the full value of the service or labor of said fugitive in the State, Territory, or District whence he escaped: and the better to enable the said **COMMISSIONERS**, when thus appointed, to execute their duties faithfully and efficiently, in **CONFORMITY WITH THE REQUIREMENTS OF THE CONSTITUTION OF THE UNITED STATES** and of this act, they are hereby authorized and empowered, within their counties respectively, to appoint, in writing under their hands, any one or more suitable persons,[4] from time to time, to execute all such warrants and other process as may be issued by them in the lawful performance of their respective duties; with authority to

---

[3] This references Federal Marshals and their deputies. Today, these persons are members of the Federal Marshal Service. One of their prime duties was/is to hunt down persons fleeing from Constitutionally mandated "justice."

[4] Non-marshals, such as fugitive **SLAVE** hunters or bounty hunters can be "deputized" and given the same power as any United States Marshal.

such **COMMISSIONERS**, or the persons to be appointed by them, to execute process as aforesaid, to summon and call to their aid the bystanders, or posse comitatus of the proper county, when necessary to ensure a faithful observance of the clause of the **CONSTITUTION** referred to, in conformity with the provisions of this act; and all good citizens are hereby commanded to aid and assist in the prompt and efficient execution of this law, whenever their services may be required, as aforesaid, for that purpose; and said warrants shall run, and be executed by said officers, any where in the State within which they are issued.

Section 6

And be it further enacted, That when [an **AFRICAN**] held to service or labor in any State or Territory of the United States, has heretofore or shall hereafter escape into another State or Territory of the United States, the person or persons to whom such service or labor may be due, or his, her, or their agent or attorney, duly authorized, by power of attorney, in writing, acknowledged and certified under the seal of some legal officer or court of the State or Territory in which the same may be executed, may pursue and reclaim such fugitive person, either by procuring a warrant from some one of the courts, judges, or **COMMISSIONERS** aforesaid, of the proper circuit, district, or county, for the apprehension of such fugitive from service or labor, or by seizing and arresting such fugitive, where the same can be done without process, and by taking, or causing such person to be taken, forthwith before such court, judge, or

COMMISSIONER, whose duty it shall be to hear and determine the case of such claimant in a summary manner; and upon satisfactory proof being made, by deposition or affidavit, in writing, to be taken and certified by such court, judge, or **COMMISSIONER**, or by other satisfactory testimony, duly taken and certified by some court, magistrate, justice of the peace, or other legal officer authorized to administer an oath and take depositions under the laws of the State or Territory from which such person owing service or labor may have escaped, with a certificate of such magistracy or other authority, as aforesaid, with the seal of the proper court or officer thereto attached, which seal shall be sufficient to establish the competency of the proof, and with proof, also by affidavit, of the identity of the person whose service or labor is claimed to be due as aforesaid, that the person so arrested does in fact owe service or labor to the person or persons claiming him or her, in the State or Territory from which such fugitive may have escaped as aforesaid, and that said person escaped, to make out and deliver to such claimant, his or her agent or attorney, a certificate setting forth the substantial facts as to the service or labor due from such fugitive to the claimant, and of his or her escape from the State or Territory in which he or she was arrested, with authority to such claimant, or his or her agent or attorney, to use such reasonable force and restraint as may be necessary, under the circumstances of the case, to take and remove such fugitive person back to the State or Territory whence he or she may have escaped as aforesaid. In no trial or hearing under this act shall the testimony of such alleged fugitive be admitted in evidence; and the certificates in this and the first [fourth] section mentioned, shall be conclusive of the right of the person or persons in whose favor granted, to remove such fugitive to the State or Territory from which he escaped, and shall prevent all molestation of such person or persons by any process issued by any court, judge, magistrate, or other person whomsoever.

Section 7

And be it further enacted, That any person who shall knowingly and willingly obstruct, hinder, or prevent such claimant, his agent or attorney, or any person or persons lawfully assisting him, her, or them, from arresting such a fugitive from service or labor, either with or without process as aforesaid, or shall rescue, or attempt to rescue, such fugitive from service or labor, from the custody of such claimant, his or her agent or attorney, or other person or persons lawfully assisting as aforesaid, when so arrested, pursuant to the authority herein given and declared; or shall aid, abet, or assist such person so owing service or labor as aforesaid, directly or indirectly, to escape from such claimant, his agent or attorney, or other person or persons legally authorized as aforesaid; or shall harbor or conceal such fugitive, so as to prevent the discovery and arrest of such person, after notice or knowledge of the fact that such person was a fugitive from service or labor as aforesaid, shall, for either of said offences, be subject to a fine not exceeding one thousand dollars, and imprisonment not exceeding six months, by indictment and conviction before the District Court of the United States for the district in which such offence may have been committed, or before the proper court of criminal jurisdiction, if committed within any one of the organized Territories of the United States; and shall moreover forfeit and pay, by way of civil damages to the party injured by such illegal conduct, the sum of one thousand dollars for each fugitive so lost as aforesaid, to be recovered by action of debt, in any of the District or Territorial Courts aforesaid, within whose jurisdiction the said offence may have been committed.

Section 8

And be it further enacted, That the marshals, their deputies, and the clerks of the said District and Territorial Courts, shall be paid, for their services, the like fees as may be allowed for similar services in other cases; and where such services are rendered exclusively in the arrest, custody, and delivery of the fugitive to the claimant, his or her agent or attorney, or where such supposed fugitive may be discharged out of custody for the want of sufficient proof as aforesaid, then such fees are to be paid in whole by such claimant, his or her agent or attorney; and in all cases where the proceedings are before a **COMMISSIONER**, he shall be entitled to a fee of ten dollars in full for his services in each case, upon the delivery of the said certificate to the claimant, his agent or attorney; or a fee of five dollars in cases where the proof shall not, in the opinion of such **COMMISSIONER**, warrant such certificate and delivery, inclusive of all services incident to such arrest and examination, to be paid, in either case, by the claimant, his or her agent or attorney. The person or persons authorized to execute the process to be issued by such **COMMISSIONER** for the arrest and detention of fugitives from service or labor as aforesaid, shall also be entitled to a fee of five dollars each for each person he or they may arrest, and take before any **COMMISSIONER** as aforesaid, at the instance and request of such claimant, with such other fees as may be deemed reasonable by such **COMMISSIONER** for such other additional services as may be necessarily performed by him or them; such as attending at the examination, keeping the fugitive in custody, and providing him with food and lodging during his detention, and until the final determination of such **COMMISSIONERS**; and, in general, for performing such other duties as may be required by such claimant, his or her attorney or agent, or **COMMISSIONER** in the premises, such fees to be made up in conformity with the fees usually charged by the officers of the courts of justice within the proper district or county, as near as may be practicable, and paid by such claimants, their agents or attorneys, whether such supposed fugitives from service or labor be ordered to be delivered to such claimant by the final determination of such **COMMISSIONER** or not.

Section 9

And be it further enacted, That, upon affidavit made by the claimant of such fugitive, his agent or attorney, after such certificate has been issued, that he has reason to apprehend that such fugitive will he rescued by force from his or their possession before he can be taken beyond the limits of the State in which the arrest is made, it shall be the duty of the officer making the arrest to retain such fugitive in his custody, and to remove him to the State whence he fled, and there to deliver him to said claimant, his agent, or attorney. And to this end, the officer aforesaid is hereby authorized and required to employ so many persons as he may deem necessary to overcome such force, and to retain them in his service so long as circumstances may require. The said officer and his assistants, while so employed, to receive the same compensation, and to be allowed the same expenses, as are now allowed by law for transportation of criminals, to be certified by the judge of the district within which the arrest is made, and paid out of the treasury of the United States.

Section 10

And be it further enacted, That when any person held to service or labor in any State or Territory, or in the District of Columbia, shall escape therefrom, the party to whom such service or labor shall be due, his, her, or their agent or attorney, may apply to any court of record therein, or judge thereof in vacation, and make satisfactory proof to such court, or judge in vacation, of the escape aforesaid, and that the person escaping owed service or labor to such party. Whereupon the court shall cause a record to be made of the matters so proved, and also a general description of the person so escaping, with such convenient certainty as may be; and a transcript of such record, authenticated by the attestation of the clerk and of the seal of the said court, being produced in any other State, Territory, or district in which the person so escaping may be found, and being exhibited to any judge, **COMMISSIONER**, or other office, authorized by the law of the United States to cause persons escaping from service or labor to be delivered up, shall be held and taken to be full and conclusive evidence of the fact of escape, and that the service or labor of the person escaping is due to the party in such record mentioned. And upon the production by the said party of other and further evidence if necessary, either oral or by affidavit, in addition to what is contained in the said record of the identity of the person escaping, he or she shall be delivered up to the claimant, And the said court, **COMMISSIONER**, judge, or other person authorized by this act to grant certificates to claimants or fugitives, shall, upon the production of the record and other evidences aforesaid, grant to such claimant a certificate of his right to take any such person identified and proved to be owing service or labor as aforesaid, which certificate shall authorize such claimant to seize or arrest and transport such person to the State or Territory from which he escaped: Provided, That nothing herein contained shall be construed as requiring the production of a transcript of such record as evidence as aforesaid. But in its absence the claim shall be heard and determined upon other satisfactory proofs, competent in law.

Approved, September 18, 1850.

Mr. Chief Justice Roger Brooke Taney
1777-1864
Wrote The United States Supreme Court's Majority
Opinion in the Case of *Scott v. Sandford*
Fifth Chief Justice of the United States (1836-1864)

The United States Supreme Court's Dred Scott Decision (1856)

Perhaps the most infamous decision ever handed down by the United States Supreme Court was its ruling in the matter of *Scott v. Sandford*. The case's origins are simple. Dred Scott, an **AFRICAN SLAVE**, was born in Virginia, (exact date unknown). Between the years 1831 and 1833, he was **SOLD** to a US Army Surgeon, James Emerson. Until Emerson's death in 1843, Scott faithfully, though unwillingly, traveled with his "Master" in typical military fashion from assignment to assignment. Many of Emerson's assignments took him to Federal territories designated as "**FREE**." Scott would later argue that his status as a **SLAVE,** while living on "**FREE SOIL,**" should have automatically made him a "**FREE**" MAN. By the time his case reached the **US Supreme Court**, and with its resultant ruling—based upon the **CONSTITUTION**—it was decided that he was *not* free regardless as to where he lived! In addition, by default, he was not even a *man!*

J.A.F Sandford, Major Emerson's brother-in-law, was a Missouri resident. Upon Mrs. Emerson's subsequent remarriage in 1846, Scott was "given" to Sandford. It was, at that time, that Scott began a legal journey that would last nearly ten years. From 1846 to 1856, Scott argued for his freedom in various state and Federal Courts. In 1856, the United States Supreme Court handed down its infamous decision in the matter of Scott's freedom. The Court defined an even larger issue—for the first time it was explicitly stated that **AFRICANS** had absolutely *no* rights! Far from establishing his status as a "**FREE**" man, the court's ruling established the principle first dictated by the Founding "Fathers" seventy years before, with the ratification of the **United States Constitution,** that **AFRICANS** were only to be considered **3/5** human! The Supreme Court's decision effected all **AFRICANS "FREE"** and **SLAVE.**

The ruling itself contains lots of legal phrases and terms. So as to help you see just exactly how the **US SUPREME COURT**—the final arbitrator of the Constitution's meaning—defined **AFRICAN HUMANITY,** to say nothing of **RIGHTS,** I purposefully placed those comments in ***BOLD ITALICS.***

What follows is the majority opinion written by **US Supreme Court** Chief Justice, Roger Brooke Taney.

The ruling reflected the hypocritical stance of the industrialized Northern States as well as the Slave Holding Southern States. It also reflected America's moral bankruptcy. "Political" considerations, informed by moral cowardice, ruled the day! A sheepish **James Buchanan**, the fifteenth **President of the United States**, perhaps summarized the mood of political cowardice when he said the following prior to the Supreme Court's Dred Scott decision:

> A difference of opinion has arisen in regard to the point of time when the people of a Territory shall decide this question [of **SLAVERY**] for themselves. This is, happily, a matter of but little practical importance. Besides, it is a judicial question, which legitimately belongs to the **Supreme Court of the United States**, before

whom it is now pending, and will, it is understood, be speedily and finally settled. *To their decision, in common with all good citizens, I shall cheerfully submit, whatever this may be.*

DRED SCOTT, PLAINTIFF IN ERROR,
v.
JOHN F. A. SANDFORD.
December Term, 1856
MR. CHIEF JUSTICE TANEY:

This case has been twice argued. After the argument at the last term, differences of opinion were found to exist among the members of the court; and as the questions in controversy are of the highest importance, and the court was at that time much pressed by the ordinary business of the term, it was deemed advisable to continue the case, and direct a re-argument on some of the points, in order that we might have an opportunity of giving to the whole subject a more deliberate consideration. It has accordingly been again argued by counsel, and considered by the court; and I now proceed to deliver its opinion.

There are two leading questions presented by the record:

1. Had the Circuit Court of the United States jurisdiction to hear and determine the case between these parties? And
2. If it had jurisdiction, is the judgment it has given erroneous or not?

The plaintiff in error, who was also the plaintiff in the court below, was, with his wife and children, held as **SLAVES** by the defendant, in the State of Missouri; and he brought this action in the Circuit Court of the United States for that district, to assert the title of himself and his family to freedom.

The declaration is in the form usually adopted in that State to try questions of this description, and contains the averment necessary to give the court jurisdiction; that he and the defendant are citizens of different States; that is, that he is a citizen of Missouri, and the defendant a citizen of New York.

The defendant pleaded in abatement to the jurisdiction of the court, that the plaintiff was not a citizen of the State of Missouri, as alleged in his declaration, being [an **AFRICAN**] of **AFRICAN** descent, whose ancestors were of pure **AFRICAN** blood, and who were brought into this country and sold as **SLAVES**.

To this plea the plaintiff demurred, and the defendant joined in demurrer. The court overruled the plea, and gave judgment that the defendant should answer over. And he thereupon put in sundry pleas in bar, upon which issues were joined; and at the trial the verdict and judgment were in his favor. Whereupon the plaintiff brought this writ of error.

Before we speak of the pleas in bar, it will be proper to dispose of the questions which have arisen on the plea in abatement.

That plea denies the right of the plaintiff to sue in a court of the United States, for the reasons therein stated.

If the question raised by it is legally before us, and the court should be of opinion that the facts stated in it disqualify the plaintiff from becoming a citizen, in the sense in which that word is used in the Constitution of the United States, then the judgment of the Circuit Court is erroneous, and must be reversed.

It is suggested, however, that this plea is not before us; and that as the judgment in the court below on this plea was in favor of the plaintiff, he does not seek to reverse it, or bring it before the court for revision by his writ of error; and also that the defendant waived this defence by pleading over, and thereby admitted the jurisdiction of the court.

But, in making this objection, we think the peculiar and limited jurisdiction of courts of the United States has not been adverted to. This peculiar and limited jurisdiction has made it necessary, in these courts, to adopt different rules and principles of pleading, so far as jurisdiction is concerned, from those which regulate courts of common law in England, and in the different States of the Union which have adopted the common-law rules.

In these last-mentioned courts, where their character and rank are analogous to that of a Circuit Court of the United States; in other words, where they are what the law terms courts of general jurisdiction; they are presumed to have jurisdiction, unless the contrary appears. No averment in the pleadings of the plaintiff is necessary, in order to give jurisdiction. If the defendant objects to it, he must plead it specially, and unless the fact on which he relies is found to be true by a jury, or admitted to be true by the plaintiff, the jurisdiction cannot be disputed in an appellate court.

Now, it is not necessary to inquire whether in courts of that description a party who pleads over in bar, when a plea to the jurisdiction has been ruled against him, does or does not waive his plea; nor whether upon a judgment in his favor on the pleas in bar, and a writ of error brought by the plaintiff, the question upon the plea in abatement would be open for revision in the appellate court. Cases that may have been decided in such courts, or rules that may have been laid down by common-law pleaders, can have no influence in the decision in this court. Because, under the Constitution and laws of the United States, the rules which govern the pleadings in its courts, in questions of jurisdiction, stand on different principles and are regulated by different laws. This difference arises, as we have said, from the peculiar character of the Government of the United States. For although it is sovereign and supreme in its appropriate sphere of action, yet it does not possess all the powers which usually belong to the sovereignty of a nation. Certain specified powers, enumerated in the Constitution, have been conferred upon it; and neither the legislative, executive, nor judicial departments of the Government can lawfully exercise any authority beyond the limits marked out by the Constitution. And in regulating the judicial department, the cases in which the courts of the United States shall have jurisdiction are particularly and specifically enumerated and defined; and they are not authorized to take cognizance of any case which does not come within the description therein specified. Hence, when a plaintiff sues in a court of the United States, it is necessary that he should show, in his pleading, that the suit he brings is within the jurisdiction of the court, and that he is entitled to sue there. And if he omits to do this, and should, by any oversight of the Circuit Court, obtain a judgment in his favor, the judgment would be reversed in the appellate court for want of jurisdiction in the court below. The jurisdiction would not be presumed, as in the case of a common-law English or State court, unless the contrary appeared. But the record, when it comes before the appellate court, must show, affirmatively, that the inferior court had authority, under the Constitution, to hear and determine the case. And if the plaintiff claims a right to sue in a Circuit Court of the United States, under that provision of the Constitution which gives jurisdiction in controversies between citizens of different States, he must distinctly aver in his pleading that they are citizens of different States; and he cannot maintain his suit without showing that fact in the pleadings.

This point was decided in the case of Bingham v. Cabot, (in 3 Dall., 382,) and ever since adhered to by the court. And in Jackson v. Ashton, (8 Pet., 148,) it was held that the objection to which it was open could not be waived by the opposite party, because consent of parties could not give jurisdiction. . . .

. . . The plea in abatement and the judgment of the court upon it, are a part of the judicial proceedings in the Circuit Court, and are there recorded as such; and a writ of error always brings up to the superior court the whole record of the proceedings in the court below. And in the case of the United States v. Smith, (11 Wheat., 172,) this court said, that the case being brought up by writ of error, the whole record was under the consideration of this court. And this being the case in the present instance, the plea in abatement is necessarily under consideration; and it becomes, therefore, our duty to decide whether the facts stated in the plea are or are not sufficient to show that the plaintiff is not entitled to sue as a citizen in a court of the United States.

This is certainly a very serious question, and one that now for the first time has been brought for decision before this court. But it is brought here by those who have a right to bring it, and it is our duty to meet it and decide it.

The question is simply this: Can [an AFRICAN], whose ancestors were imported into this country, and sold as SLAVES, become a member of the political community formed and brought into existence by the Constitution of the United States, and as such become entitled to all the rights, and privileges, and immunities, guarantied by that instrument to the citizen? One of which rights is the privilege of suing in a court of the United States in the cases specified in the Constitution.

It will be observed, that the plea applies to that class of persons only whose ancestors were [AFRICANS] of the AFRICAN race, and imported into this country, and sold and held as SLAVES. The only matter in issue before the court, therefore, is, whether the descendants of such SLAVES, when they shall be emancipated, or who are born of parents who had become free before their birth, are citizens of a State, in the sense in which the word citizen is used in the Constitution of the United States.[1] And this being the only matter in dispute on the pleadings, the court must be understood as speaking in this opinion of that class only, that is, of those persons who are the descendants of AFRICANS who were imported into this country, and sold as SLAVES.

The situation of this population was altogether unlike that of the Indian race. The latter, it is true, formed no part of the colonial communities, and never amalgamated with them in social connections or in government. But although they were uncivilized, they were yet a free and independent people,

---

[1] Taney raises the following point—can persons of **AFRICAN** descent, whether born **SLAVE** or "**FREE**" be considered citizens, in the sense that the (so-called) Founding Fathers meant it.

associated together in nations or tribes, and governed by their own laws. Many of these political communities were situated in territories to which the White race claimed the ultimate right of dominion. But that claim was acknowledged to be subject to the right of the Indians to occupy it as long as they thought proper, and neither the English nor colonial Governments claimed or exercised any dominion over the tribe or nation by whom it was occupied, nor claimed the right to the possession of the territory, until the tribe or nation consented to cede it. These Indian Governments were regarded and treated as foreign Governments, as much so as if an ocean had separated the red man from the White; and their freedom has constantly been acknowledged, from the time of the first emigration to the English colonies to the present day, by the different Governments which succeeded each other. Treaties have been negotiated with them, and their alliance sought for in war; and the people who compose these Indian political communities have always been treated as foreigners not living under our Government. It is true that the course of events has brought the Indian tribes within the limits of the United States under subjection to the White race; and it has been found necessary, for their sake as well as our own, to regard them as in a state of pupilage, and to legislate to a certain extent over them and the territory they occupy. But they may, without doubt, like the subjects of any other foreign Government, be naturalized by the authority of Congress, and become citizens of a State, and of the United States; and if an individual should leave his nation or tribe, and take up his abode among the White population, he would be entitled to all the rights and privileges which would belong to an emigrant from any other foreign people.

We proceed to examine the case as presented by the pleadings.
The words 'people of the United States' and 'citizens' are synonymous terms, and mean the same thing.[2] They both describe the political body who, according to our republican institutions, form the sovereignty, and who hold the power and conduct the Government through their representatives. They are what we familiarly call the 'sovereign people,' and every citizen is one of this people, and a constituent member of this sovereignty. The question before us is, whether the class of persons described in the plea in abatement compose a portion of this people, and are constituent members of this sovereignty? We think they are not, and that they are not included, and were not intended to be included, under the word 'citizens' in the Constitution, and can therefore claim none of the rights and privileges which that instrument provides for and secures to citizens of the United States. On the contrary, they were at that time considered as a subordinate and inferior class of beings, who had been subjugated by the dominant race, and, whether emancipated or not, yet remained subject to their authority, and had no rights or privileges but such as those who held the power and the Government might choose to grant them.

It is not the province of the court to decide upon the justice or injustice, the policy or impolicy, of these laws. The decision of that question belonged to the political or law-making power; to those who formed the sovereignty and framed the Constitution. The duty of the court is, to interpret the instrument they have

---

[2] Since the Chief Justice looks upon the terms "**PEOPLE**" and "**CITIZEN**" are synonymous, he is building a carefully crafted argument that will "prove" that **AFRICANS** are neither **HUMAN** or equal partners with *WHITE* "CITIZENS."

framed, with the best lights we can obtain on the subject, and to administer it as we find it, according to its true intent and meaning when it was adopted.

In discussing this question, we must not confound the rights of citizenship which a State may confer within its own limits, and the rights of citizenship as a member of the Union. It does not by any means follow, because he has all the rights and privileges of a citizen of a State, that he must be a citizen of the United States. He may have all of the rights and privileges of the citizen of a State, and yet not be entitled to the rights and privileges of a citizen in any other State. For, previous to the adoption of the Constitution of the United States, every State had the undoubted right to confer on whomsoever it pleased the character of citizen, and to endow him with all its rights. But this character of course was confined to the boundaries of the State, and gave him no rights or privileges in other States beyond those secured to him by the laws of nations and the comity of States. Nor have the several States surrendered the power of conferring these rights and privileges by adopting the Constitution of the United States. Each State may still confer them upon an alien, or any one it thinks proper, or upon any class or description of persons; yet he would not be a citizen in the sense in which that word is used in the Constitution of the United States, nor entitled to sue as such in one of its courts, nor to the privileges and immunities of a citizen in the other States. The rights which he would acquire would be restricted to the State which gave them. The Constitution has conferred on Congress the right to establish an uniform rule of naturalization, and this right is evidently exclusive, and has always been held by this court to be so. Consequently, no State, since the adoption of the Constitution, can by naturalizing an alien invest him with the rights and privileges secured to a citizen of a State under the Federal Government, although, so far as the State alone was concerned, he would undoubtedly be entitled to the rights of a citizen, and clothed with all the rights and immunities which the Constitution and laws of the State attached to that character.

It is very clear, therefore, that no State can, by any act or law of its own, passed since the adoption of the Constitution, introduce a new member into the political community created by the Constitution of the United States. It cannot make him a member of this community by making him a member of its own. And for the same reason it cannot introduce any person, or description of persons, who were not intended to be embraced in this new political family, which the Constitution brought into existence, but were intended to be excluded from it.[3]

The question then arises, whether the provisions of the Constitution, in relation to the personal rights and privileges to which the citizen of a State should be entitled, embraced the **AFRICAN** race, at that time in this country, or who might afterwards be imported, who had then or should afterwards be made free in any State; and to put it in the power of a single State to make him a citizen of the United States, and endue him with the full rights of citizenship in every other State without their consent? Does the Constitution of the United States act upon him whenever he shall be made free under the laws of a State, and raised there to the rank of a citizen, and immediately

---

[3] **AFRICANS** *were not* considered **CITIZENS** when the **CONSTITUION** was adopted; it is impossible to consider them so at this point. In other words, it's too late!

clothe him with all the privileges of a citizen in every other State, and in its own courts?

The court thinks the affirmative of these propositions cannot be maintained. And if it cannot, the plaintiff in error could not be a citizen of the State of Missouri, within the meaning of the Constitution of the United States, and, consequently, was not entitled to sue in its courts.

It is true, every person, and every class and description of persons, who were at the time of the adoption of the Constitution recognised as citizens in the several States, became also citizens of this new political body; but none other; it was formed by them, and for them and their posterity, but for no one else. And the personal rights and privileges guarantied to citizens of this new sovereignty were intended to embrace those only who were then members of the several State communities, or who should afterwards by birthright or otherwise become members, according to the provisions of the Constitution and the principles on which it was founded. It was the union of those who were at that time members of distinct and separate political communities into one political family, whose power, for certain specified purposes, was to extend over the whole territory of the United States. And it gave to each citizen rights and privileges outside of his State which he did not before possess, and placed him in every other State upon a perfect equality with its own citizens as to rights of person and rights of property; it made him a citizen of the United States.

It becomes necessary, therefore, to determine who were citizens of the several States when the Constitution was adopted. And in order to do this, we must recur to the Governments and institutions of the thirteen colonies, when they separated from

Great Britain and formed new sovereignties, and took their places in the family of independent nations. We must inquire who, at that time, were recognised as the people or citizens of a State, whose rights and liberties had been outraged by the English Government; and who declared their independence, and assumed the powers of Government to defend their rights by force of arms.

In the opinion of the court, the legislation and histories of the times, and the language used in the DECLARATION OF INDEPENDENCE, show, that neither the class of persons who had been imported as SLAVES, nor their descendants, whether they had become free or not, were then acknowledged as a part of the people, nor intended to be included in the general words used in that memorable instrument.[4]

It is difficult at this day to realize the state of public opinion in relation to that unfortunate race, which prevailed in the civilized and enlightened portions of the world at the time of the Declaration of Independence, and when the Constitution of the United States was framed and adopted. But the public history of every European nation displays it in a manner too plain to be mistaken.

---

[4] The **DECLARATION OF INDEPENDENCE** deliberately *EXCLUDED* persons of **AFRICAN** descent as persons "worthy" of **FREEDOM**. This applied to persons that were/are **SLAVE** and "**FREE**."

[AFRICANS] had for more than a century before been regarded as beings of an inferior order, and altogether unfit to associate with the White race, either in social or political relations; and so far inferior, that they had no rights which the White man was bound to respect; and that the [AFRICAN] might justly and lawfully be reduced to SLAVERY for his benefit. He was bought and sold, and treated as an ordinary article of merchandise and traffic, whenever a profit could be made by it. This opinion was at that time fixed and universal in the civilized portion of the White race. It was regarded as an axiom in morals as well as in politics, which no one thought of disputing, or supposed to be open to dispute; and men in every grade and position in society daily and habitually acted upon it in their private pursuits, as well as in matters of public concern, without doubting for a moment the correctness of this opinion.

And in no nation was this opinion more firmly fixed or more uniformly acted upon than by the English Government and English people. They not only seized them on the coast of AFRICA, and sold them or held them in SLAVERY for their own use; but they took them as ordinary articles of merchandise to every country where they could make a profit on them, and were far more extensively engaged in this commerce than any other nation in the world. [5]

---

[5] This is perhaps one of the more infamous passages in Chief Justice Taney's document. Based upon his careful reading of British and Colonial tradition, the relationship between **AFRICANS** and Europeans, and his understanding of the intent of the framers of the **CONSTITUION**, he baldly states that **AFRICANS** have absolutely no rights that a **WHITE** is bound to respect.

The opinion thus entertained and acted upon in England was naturally impressed upon the colonies they founded on this side of the Atlantic. And, accordingly, [an **AFRICAN**] was *regarded by them as an article of property*, and held, and bought and sold as such, in every one of the thirteen colonies which united in the Declaration of Independence, and afterwards formed the Constitution of the United States. The **SLAVES** were more or less numerous in the different colonies, as **SLAVE** labor was found more or less profitable. But no one seems to have doubted the correctness of the prevailing opinion of the time.

The legislation of the different colonies furnishes positive and indisputable proof of this fact. . . .

The province of Maryland, in 1717, (ch. 13, s. 5,) passed a law declaring 'that if any free **[AFRICAN]** or mulatto intermarry with any White woman, or if any White man shall intermarry with any **[AFRICAN]** or mulatto woman, such **[AFRICAN]** or mulatto shall become a **SLAVE** during life, excepting mulattoes born of White women, who, for such intermarriage, shall only become servants for seven years, to be disposed of as the justices of the county court, where such marriage so happens, shall think fit; to be applied by them towards the support of a public school within the said county. And any White man or White woman who shall intermarry as aforesaid, with any **[AFRICAN]** or mulatto, such White man or White woman shall become servants during the term of seven years, and shall be disposed of by the justices as aforesaid, and be applied to the uses aforesaid.'

The other colonial law to which we refer was passed by Massachusetts in 1705, (chap. 6.) It is entitled 'An act for the better preventing of a spurious and mixed issue,' &c.; and it provides, that 'if any **[AFRICAN]** or mulatto shall presume to smite or strike any person of the English or other Christian nation, such **[AFRICAN]** or mulatto shall be severely whipped, at the discretion of the justices before whom the offender shall be convicted.'. . .

We give both of these laws in the words used by the respective legislative bodies, because the language in which they are framed, as well as the provisions contained in them, show, too plainly to be misunderstood, the degraded condition of this unhappy race. They were still in force when the Revolution began, and are a faithful index to the state of feeling towards the class of persons of whom they speak, and of the position they occupied throughout the thirteen colonies, in the eyes and thoughts of the men who framed the Declaration of Independence and established the State Constitutions and Governments. They show that a perpetual and impassable barrier was intended to be erected between the White race and the one which they had reduced to **SLAVERY**, and governed as subjects with absolute and despotic power, and which they then looked upon as so far below them in the scale of created beings, that intermarriages between White persons and **[AFRICANS]** or mulattoes were regarded as unnatural and immoral, and punished as crimes, not only in the parties, but in the person who joined them in marriage. *And no distinction in this respect was made between the free [AFRICAN] or mulatto and the **SLAVE**, but this stigma, of the deepest degradation, was fixed upon the whole race.*

We refer to these historical facts for the purpose of showing the fixed opinions concerning that race, upon which the statesmen of that day spoke and acted. It is necessary to do this, in order to determine whether the general terms used in the Constitution of the United States, as to the rights of man and the rights of the people, was intended to include them, or to give to them or their posterity the benefit of any of its provisions.

But there are two clauses in the Constitution which point directly and specifically to the [AFRICAN] race as a separate class of persons, and show clearly that they were not regarded as a portion of the people or citizens of the Government then formed.

One of these clauses reserves to each of the thirteen States the right to import **SLAVES** until the year 1808, if it thinks proper. And the importation which it thus sanctions was unquestionably of persons of the race of which we are speaking, as the traffic in **SLAVES** in the United States had always been confined to them. And by the other provision the States pledged themselves to each other to maintain the right of property and master, by delivering up to him any **SLAVE** who may have escaped from his service, and be found within their respective territories. By the first above-mentioned clause, therefore, the right to purchase and hold this property is directly sanctioned and authorized for twenty years by the people who framed the Constitution. And by the second, they pledge themselves to maintain and uphold the right of the master in the manner specified, as long as the government they then formed should endure. And these two provisions show, conclusively, that neither the description of persons therein referred to, nor their descendants, were embraced in any of the other provisions of the Constitution; for certainly these two clauses were not intended to confer on them or their posterity the blessings of liberty, or any of the personal rights so carefully provided for the citizen.

No one of that race had ever migrated to the United States voluntarily; all of them had been brought here as ARTICLES OF MERCHANDISE. The number that had been emancipated at that time were but few in comparison with those held in **SLAVERY**; and they were identified in the public mind with the race to which they belonged, and regarded as a part of the **SLAVE** population rather than the free. It is obvious that they were not even in the minds of the framers of the Constitution when they were conferring special rights and privileges upon the citizens of a State in every other part of the Union.

Indeed, when we look to the condition of this race in the several States at the time, it is impossible to believe that these rights and privileges were intended to be extended to them.

It is very true, that in that portion of the Union where the labor of the [**AFRICAN**] race was found to be unsuited to the climate and unprofitable to the master, but few **SLAVES** were held at the time of the Declaration of Independence; and when the Constitution was adopted, it had entirely worn out in one of them, and measures had been taken for its gradual abolition in several others. But this change had not been produced by any change of opinion in relation to this race; but because it was discovered, from experience, that **SLAVE** labor was unsuited to the climate and productions of these States: for some of the States, where it had ceased or nearly ceased to exist, were actively engaged in the **SLAVE** trade, procuring cargoes on the coast of **AFRICA**, and transporting them for sale to those parts of the Union where their labor was found to be profitable, and suited to the climate and productions. And this traffic was openly carried on, and fortunes accumulated by it, without reproach from the people of the States where they resided. And

it can hardly be supposed that, in the States where it was then countenanced in its worst form--that is, in the seizure and transportation--the people could have regarded those who were emancipated as entitled to equal rights with themselves. And we may here again refer, in support of this proposition, to the plain and unequivocal language of the laws of the several States, some passed after the Declaration of Independence and before the Constitution was adopted, and some since the Government went into operation. We need not refer, on this point, particularly to the laws of the present **SLAVEHOLDING** States. Their statute books are full of provisions in relation to this class, in the same spirit with the Maryland law which we have before quoted. *They have continued to treat them as an inferior class, and to subject them to strict police regulations, drawing a broad line of distinction between the citizen and the SLAVE races, and legislating in relation to them upon the same principle which prevailed at the time of the Declaration of Independence.* As relates to these States, it is too plain for argument, that they have never been regarded as a part of the people or citizens of the State, nor supposed to possess any political rights which the dominant race might not withhold or grant at their pleasure. And as long ago as 1822, *the Court of Appeals of Kentucky decided that free [AFRICANS] and mulattoes were not citizens within the meaning of the Constitution of the United States; and the correctness of this decision is recognized, and the same doctrine affirmed, in 1 Meigs's Tenn. Reports, 331.*
And if we turn to the legislation of the States where **SLAVERY** had worn out, or measures taken for its speedy abolition, we

shall find the same opinions and principles equally fixed and equally acted upon.

Thus, Massachusetts, in 1786, passed a law similar to the colonial one of which we have spoken. The law of 1786, like the law of 1705, forbids the marriage of any White person with any **[AFRICAN]**, Indian, or mulatto, and inflicts a penalty of fifty pounds upon any one who shall join them in marriage; and declares all such marriage absolutely null and void, and degrades thus the unhappy issue of the marriage by fixing upon it the stain of bastardy. And this mark of degradation was renewed, and again impressed upon the race, in the careful and deliberate preparation of their revised code published in 1836. This code forbids any person from joining in marriage any White person with any Indian, **[AFRICAN]**, or mulatto, and subjects the party who shall offend in this respect, to imprisonment, not exceeding six months, in the common jail, or to hard labor, and to a fine of not less than fifty nor more than two hundred dollars; and, like the law of 1786, it declares the marriage to be absolutely null and void. It will be seen that the punishment is increased by the code upon the person who shall marry them, by adding imprisonment to a pecuniary penalty.

So, too, in Connecticut. We refer more particularly to the legislation of this State, because it was not only among the first to put an end to **SLAVERY** within its own territory, but was the first to fix a mark of reprobation upon the **AFRICAN SLAVE** trade. The law last mentioned was passed in October, 1788, about nine months after the State had ratified and adopted the present Constitution of the United States; and by that law it prohibited its own citizens, under severe penalties, from engaging in the trade, and declared all policies of insurance on the vessel or cargo made in the State to be null and void. But, up to the time of the adoption of the Constitution, there is nothing in the legislation of the State indicating any change of opinion as to the relative rights and position of the White and black races in this country, or indicating that it meant to place the latter, when free, upon a level with its citizens. And certainly nothing which would have led the **SLAVEHOLDING** States to suppose, that Connecticut designed to claim for them, under the new Constitution, the equal rights and privileges and rank of citizens in every other State.

The first step taken by Connecticut upon this subject was as early as 1774, when it passed an act forbidding the further importation of **SLAVES** into the State. But the section containing the prohibition is introduced by the following preamble:

'And whereas the increase of **SLAVES** in this State is injurious to the poor, and inconvenient.'

This recital would appear to have been carefully introduced, in order to prevent any misunderstanding of the motive which induced the Legislature to pass the law, and places it distinctly upon the interest and convenience of the White population--excluding the inference that it might have been intended in any degree for the benefit of the other.

And in the act of 1784, by which the issue of **SLAVES**, born after the time therein mentioned, were to be free at a certain age, the section is again introduced by a preamble assigning a similar motive for the act. It is in these words:

'Whereas sound policy requires that the abolition of **SLAVERY** should be effected as soon as may be consistent with the rights of individuals, and the public safety and welfare'--showing that the right of property in the master was to be protected, and that the measure was one of policy, and to prevent the injury and inconvenience, to the Whites, of a **SLAVE** population in the State.

And still further pursuing its legislation, we find that in the same statute passed in 1774, which prohibited the further importation of **SLAVES** into the State, there is also a provision by which any **[AFRICAN]**, Indian, or mulatto servant, who was found wandering out of the town or place to which he belonged, without a written pass such as is therein described, was made liable to be seized by any one, and taken before the next authority to be examined and delivered up to his master--who was required to pay the charge which had accrued thereby. And a subsequent section of the same law provides, that if any free **[AFRICAN]** shall travel without such pass, and shall be stopped, seized, or taken up, he shall pay all charges arising thereby. And this law was in full operation when the Constitution of the United States was adopted, and was not repealed till 1797. So that up to that time free **[AFRICANS]** and mulattoes were associated with servants and **SLAVES** in the police regulations established by the laws of the State.

And again, in 1833, Connecticut passed another law, which made it penal to set up or establish any school in that State for the instruction of persons of the **AFRICAN** race not inhabitants of the State, or to instruct or teach in any such school or institution, or board or harbor for that purpose, any such person, without the previous consent in writing of the civil authority of the town in which such school or institution might be.

And it appears by the case of Crandall v. The State, reported in 10 Conn. Rep., 340, that upon an information filed against

Prudence Crandall for a violation of this law, one of the points raised in the defence was, that the law was a violation of the Constitution of the United States; and that the persons instructed, although of the **AFRICAN** race, were citizens of other States, and therefore entitled to the rights and privileges of citizens in the State of Connecticut. But *Chief Justice Dagget, before whom the case was tried, held, that persons of that description were not citizens of a State, within the meaning of the word citizen in the Constitution of the United States, and were not therefore entitled to the privileges and immunities of citizens in other States.*

The case was carried up to the Supreme Court of Errors of the State, and the question fully argued there. But the case went off upon another point, and no opinion was expressed on this question.

We have made this particular examination into the legislative and judicial action of Connecticut, because, from the early hostility it displayed to the **SLAVE** trade on the coast of **AFRICA**, we may expect to find the laws of that State as lenient and favorable to the subject race as those of any other State in the Union; and if we find that at the time the Constitution was adopted, they were not even there raised to the rank of citizens, but were still held and treated as property, and the laws relating to them passed with reference altogether to the interest and convenience of the White race, we shall hardly find them elevated to a higher rank anywhere else.

A brief notice of the laws of two other States, and we shall pass on to other considerations.

By the laws of New Hampshire, collected and finally passed in 1815, no one was permitted to be enrolled in the militia of the

State, but free White citizens; and the same provision is found in a subsequent collection of the laws, made in 1855. Nothing could more strongly mark the entire repudiation of the **AFRICAN** race. The alien is excluded, because, being born in a foreign country, he cannot be a member of the community until he is naturalized. *But why are the AFRICAN race, born in the State, not permitted to share in one of the highest duties of the citizen? The answer is obvious; he is not, by the institutions and laws of the State, numbered among its people. He forms no part of the sovereignty of the State, and is not therefore called on to uphold and defend it.*
Again, in 1822, Rhode Island, in its revised code, passed a law forbidding persons who were authorized to join persons in marriage, from joining in marriage any White person with any [AFRICAN], Indian, or mulatto, under the penalty of two hundred dollars, and declaring all such marriages absolutely null and void; and the same law was again re-enacted in its revised code of 1844. So that, down to the last-mentioned period, the strongest mark of inferiority and degradation was fastened upon the **AFRICAN** race in that State.
It would be impossible to enumerate and compress in the space usually allotted to an opinion of a court, the various laws, marking the condition of this race, which were passed from time to time after the Revolution, and before and since the adoption of the Constitution of the United States. In addition to those already referred to, it is sufficient to say, that Chancellor Kent, whose accuracy and research no one will question, states in the sixth edition of his Commentaries, (published in 1848, 2 vol., 258, note b,) that in no part of the country except Maine, did the

AFRICAN race, in point of fact, participate equally with the Whites in the exercise of civil and political rights. The legislation of the States therefore shows, in a manner not to be mistaken, the inferior and subject condition of that race at the time the Constitution was adopted, and long afterwards, throughout the thirteen States by which that instrument was framed; and it is hardly consistent with the respect due to these States, to suppose that they regarded at that time, as fellow-citizens and members of the sovereignty, a class of beings whom they had thus stigmatized; whom, as we are bound, out of respect to the State sovereignties, to assume they had deemed it just and necessary thus to stigmatize, and upon whom they had impressed such deep and enduring marks of inferiority and degradation; or, that when they met in convention to form the Constitution, they looked upon them as a portion of their constituents, or designed to include them in the provisions so carefully inserted for the security and protection of the liberties and rights of their citizens. It cannot be supposed that they intended to secure to them rights, and privileges, and rank, in the new political body throughout the Union, which every one of them denied within the limits of its own dominion. More especially, it cannot be believed that the large **SLAVE** holding States regarded them as included in the word citizens, or would have consented to a Constitution which might compel them to receive them in that character from another State. For if they were so received, and entitled to the privileges and immunities of citizens, it would exempt them from the operation of the special laws and from the police regulations which they considered to be necessary for their own safety. It would give to persons of the **[AFRICAN]** race, who were recognised as citizens in any one State of the Union, the right to enter every other State whenever they pleased, singly or in companies, without pass or passport, and without obstruction, to sojourn there as long as they pleased, to go where they pleased at every hour of the day or night without molestation, unless they committed some violation of law for which a White man would be punished; and it would give them the full liberty of speech in public and in private upon all subjects upon which its own citizens might speak; to hold public meetings upon political affairs, and to keep and carry arms wherever they went. And all of this would be done in the face of the subject race of the same color, both free and **SLAVES**, and inevitably producing discontent and insubordination among them, and endangering the peace and safety of the State.

It is impossible, it would seem, to believe that the great men of the **SLAVEHOLDING** States, who took so large a share in framing the Constitution of the United States, and exercised so much influence in procuring its adoption, could have been so forgetful or regardless of their own safety and the safety of those who trusted and confided in them.

Besides, this want of foresight and care would have been utterly inconsistent with the caution displayed in providing for the admission of new members into this political family. For, when they gave to the citizens of each State the privileges and immunities of citizens in the several States, they at the same time took from the several States the power of naturalization, and confined that power exclusively to the Federal Government. No State was willing to permit another State to determine who should or should not be admitted as one of its citizens, and entitled to demand equal rights and privileges with their own people, within their own territories. The right of naturalization was therefore, with one accord, surrendered by the States, and confided to the Federal Government. And this power granted to Congress to establish a uniform rule of naturalization is, by the well-understood meaning of the word, confined to persons born in a foreign country, under a foreign Government. It is not a power to raise to the rank of a citizen any one born in the United States, who, from birth or parentage, by the laws of the country, belongs to an inferior and subordinate class. And when we find the States guarding themselves from the indiscreet or improper admission by other States of emigrants from other countries, by giving the power exclusively to Congress, we cannot fail to see that they could never have left with the States a much more important power--that is, the power of transforming into citizens a numerous class of persons, who in that character would be much more dangerous to the peace and safety of a large portion of the Union, than the few foreigners one of the States might improperly naturalize. The Constitution upon its adoption obviously took from the States all power by any subsequent legislation to introduce as a citizen into the political family of the United States any one, no matter where he was born, or what might be his character or condition; and it gave to Congress the power to confer this character upon those only who were born outside of the dominions of the United States. And no law of a State, therefore, passed since the Constitution was adopted, can give any right of citizenship outside of its own territory.

A clause similar to the one in the Constitution, in relation to the rights and immunities of citizens of one State in the other States, was contained in the Articles of Confederation. But there is a difference of language, which is worthy of note. The provision

in the Articles of Confederation was, 'that the free inhabitants of each of the States, paupers, vagabonds, and fugitives from justice, excepted, should be entitled to all the privileges and immunities of free citizens in the several States.'
It will be observed, that under this Confederation, each State had the right to decide for itself, and in its own tribunals, whom it would acknowledge as a free inhabitant of another State. The term free inhabitant, in the generality of its terms, would certainly include one of the **AFRICAN** race who had been manumitted. But no example, we think, can be found of his admission to all the privileges of citizenship in any State of the Union after these Articles were formed, and while they continued in force. *And, notwithstanding the generality of the words 'free inhabitants,' it is very clear that, according to their accepted meaning in that day, they did not include the AFRICAN race, whether free or not: for the fifth section of the ninth article provides that Congress should have the power 'to agree upon the number of land forces to be raised, and to make requisitions from each State for its quota in proportion to the number of White inhabitants in such State, which requisition should be binding.'*
Words could hardly have been used which more strongly mark the line of distinction between the citizen and the subject; the free and the subjugated races. The latter were not even counted when the inhabitants of a State were to be embodied in proportion to its numbers for the general defence. And it cannot for a moment be supposed, that a class of persons thus separated and rejected from those who formed the sovereignty of the States, were yet intended to be included under the words 'free

inhabitants,' in the preceding article, to whom privileges and immunities were so carefully secured in every State. But although this clause of the Articles of Confederation is the same in principle with that inserted in the Constitution, yet the comprehensive word inhabitant, which might be construed to include an emancipated **SLAVE**, is omitted; and the privilege is confined to citizens of the State. And this alteration in words would hardly have been made, unless a different meaning was intended to be conveyed, or a possible doubt removed. The just and fair inference is, that as this privilege was about to be placed under the protection of the General Government, and the words expounded by its tribunals, and all power in relation to it taken from the State and its courts, it was deemed prudent to describe with precision and caution the persons to whom this high privilege was given--and the word citizen was on that account substituted for the words free inhabitant. The word citizen excluded, and no doubt intended to exclude, foreigners who had not become citizens of some one of the States when the Constitution was adopted; and also every description of persons who were not fully recognised as citizens in the several States. This, upon any fair construction of the instruments to which we have referred, was evidently the object and purpose of this change of words.

To all this mass of proof we have still to add, that Congress has repeatedly legislated upon the same construction of the Constitution that we have given. Three laws, two of which were passed almost immediately after the Government went into operation, will be abundantly sufficient to show this. The two first are particularly worthy of notice, because many of the men who assisted in framing the Constitution, and took an active part in procuring its adoption, were then in the halls of legislation, and certainly understood what they meant when they used the words 'people of the United States' and 'citizen' in that well-considered instrument.

The first of these acts is the naturalization law, which was passed at the second session of the first Congress, March 26, 1790, and confines the right of becoming citizens 'to aliens being free White persons.'

Now, the Constitution does not limit the power of Congress in this respect to White persons. And they may, if they think proper, authorize the naturalization of any one, of any color, who was born under allegiance to another Government. *But the language of the law above quoted, shows that citizenship at that time was perfectly understood to be confined to the White race; and that they alone constituted the sovereignty in the Government.*

Congress might, as we before said, have authorized the naturalization of Indians, because they were aliens and foreigners. But, in their then untutored and savage state, no one would have thought of admitting them as citizens in a civilized community. And, moreover, the atrocities they had but recently committed, when they were the allies of Great Britain in the Revolutionary war, were yet fresh in the recollection of the people of the United States, and they were even then guarding themselves against the threatened renewal of Indian hostilities. No one supposed then that any Indian would ask for, or was capable of enjoying, the privileges of an American citizen, and the word White was not used with any particular reference to them.

Neither was it used with any reference to the AFRICAN race imported into or born in this country; because Congress had no power to naturalize them, and therefore there was no necessity for using particular words to exclude them.

It would seem to have been used merely because it followed out the line of division which the Constitution has drawn between the citizen race, who formed and held the Government, and the **AFRICAN** race, which they held in subjection and **SLAVERY**, and governed at their own pleasure.

Another of the early laws of which we have spoken, is the first militia law, which was passed in 1792, at the first session of the second Congress. The language of this law is equally plain and significant with the one just mentioned. It directs that every 'free able-bodied White male citizen' shall be enrolled in the militia. The word White is evidently used to exclude the **AFRICAN** race, and the word 'citizen' to exclude unnaturalized foreigners; the latter forming no part of the sovereignty, owing it no allegiance, and therefore under no obligation to defend it. The **AFRICAN** race, however, born in the country, did owe allegiance to the Government, whether they were **SLAVE** or free; but it is repudiated, and rejected from the duties and obligations of citizenship in marked language.

The third act to which we have alluded is even still more decisive; it was passed as late as 1813, (2 Stat., 809,) and it provides: 'That from and after the termination of the war in which the United States are now engaged with Great Britain, it shall not be lawful to employ, on board of any public or private vessels of the United States, any person or persons except citizens of the United States, or persons of color, natives of the United States.

Here the line of distinction is drawn in express words. Persons of color, in the judgment of Congress, were not included in the word citizens, and they are described as another and different class of persons, and authorized to be employed, if born in the United States.

And even as late as 1820, (chap. 104, sec. 8,) in the charter to the city of Washington, the corporation is authorized 'to restrain and prohibit the nightly and other disorderly meetings of **SLAVES**, free [**AFRICANS**], and mulattoes,' thus associating them together in its legislation; and after prescribing the punishment that may be inflicted on the **SLAVES**, proceeds in the following words: 'And to punish such free [**AFRICANS**] and mulattoes by penalties not exceeding twenty dollars for any one offence; and in case of the inability of any such free [**AFRICAN**] or mulatto to pay any such penalty and cost thereon, to cause him or her to be confined to labor for any time not exceeding six calendar months.' And in a subsequent part of the same section, the act authorizes the corporation 'to prescribe the terms and conditions upon which free [**AFRICANS**] and mulattoes may reside in the city.'

This law, like the laws of the States, shows that this class of persons were governed by special legislation directed expressly to them, and always connected with provisions for the government of **SLAVES**, and not with those for the government of free White citizens. And after such an uniform course of legislation as we have stated, by the colonies, by the States, and by Congress, running through a period of more than a century, it would seem that to call persons thus marked and stigmatized, 'citizens' of the United States, 'fellow-citizens,' a constituent part of the sovereignty, would be an abuse of terms, and not calculated to exalt the character of an American citizen in the eyes of other nations.

The conduct of the Executive Department of the Government has been in perfect harmony upon this subject with this course of legislation. *The question was brought officially before the late William Wirt, when he was the Attorney General of the United States, in 1821, and he decided that the words 'citizens of the United States' were used in the acts of Congress in the same sense as in the Constitution; and that free persons of color were not citizens, within the meaning of the Constitution and laws; and this opinion has been confirmed by that of the late Attorney General, Caleb Cushing, in a recent case, and acted upon by the Secretary of State, who refused to grant passports to them as 'citizens of the United States.'*

But it is said that a person may be a citizen, and entitled to that character, although he does not possess all the rights which may belong to other citizens; as, for example, the right to vote, or to hold particular offices; and that yet, when he goes into another State, he is entitled to be recognised there as a citizen, although the State may measure his rights by the rights which it allows to persons of a like character or class resident in the State, and refuse to him the full rights of citizenship.

This argument overlooks the language of the provision in the Constitution of which we are speaking.

Undoubtedly, a person may be a citizen, that is, a member of the community who form the sovereignty, although he exercises no share of the political power, and is incapacitated from holding particular offices. Women and minors, who form a part of the political family, cannot vote; and when a property qualification is required to vote or hold a particular office, those who have not the necessary qualification cannot vote or hold the office, yet they are citizens.

So, too, a person may be entitled to vote by the law of the State, who is not a citizen even of the State itself. And in some of the States of the Union foreigners not naturalized are allowed to vote. And *the State may give the right to free [AFRICANS] and mulattoes, but that does not make them citizens of the State, and still less of the United States.* And the provision in the Constitution giving privileges and immunities in other States, does not apply to them.

Neither does it apply to a person who, being the citizen of a State, migrates to another State. For then he becomes subject to the laws of the State in which he lives, and he is no longer a citizen of the State from which he removed. And the State in which he resides may then, unquestionably, determine his status or condition, and place him among the class of persons who are not recognised as citizens, but belong to an inferior and subject race; and may deny him the privileges and immunities enjoyed by its citizens.

But so far as mere rights of person are concerned, the provision in question is confined to citizens of a State who are temporarily in another State without taking up their residence there. It gives them no political rights in the State, as to voting or holding office, or in any other respect. For a citizen of one State has no right to participate in the government of another. But if he ranks as a citizen in the State to which he belongs, within the meaning of the Constitution of the United States, then, whenever he goes into another State, the Constitution clothes him, as to the rights of person, will all the privileges and immunities which belong to citizens of the State. And if persons of the **AFRICAN** race are citizens of a State, and of the United States, they would be entitled to all of these privileges and immunities in every State, and the State could not restrict them; for they would hold these privileges and immunities under the paramount authority of the Federal Government, and its courts would be bound to maintain and enforce them, the Constitution and laws of the State to the contrary notwithstanding. And if the States could limit or restrict them, or place the party in an inferior grade, this clause of the Constitution would be unmeaning, and could have no operation; and would give no rights to the citizen when in another State. He would have none but what the State itself chose to allow him. This is evidently not the construction or meaning of the clause in question. It guaranties rights to the citizen, and the State cannot withhold them. And these rights are of a character and would lead to consequences which make it absolutely certain that the **AFRICAN** race were not included under the name of citizens of a State, and were not in the contemplation of the framers of the Constitution when these privileges and immunities were provided for the protection of the citizen in other States. . . .

. . . *[T]he court is of opinion, that, upon the facts stated in the plea in abatement, Dred Scott was not a citizen of Missouri within the meaning of the Constitution of the United States, and not entitled as such to sue in its courts; and, consequently, that the Circuit Court had no jurisdiction of the case, and that the judgment on the plea in abatement is erroneous.*

We are aware that doubts are entertained by some of the members of the court, whether the plea in abatement is legally before the court upon this writ of error; but if that plea is regarded as waived, or out of the case upon any other ground, yet the question as to the jurisdiction of the Circuit Court is presented on the face of the bill of exception itself, taken by the plaintiff at the trial; for he admits that he and his wife were born **SLAVES**, but endeavors to make out his title to freedom and citizenship by showing that they were taken by their owner to certain places, hereinafter mentioned, where **SLAVERY** could not by law exist, and that they thereby became free, and upon their return to Missouri became citizens of that State.

Now, if the removal of which he speaks did not give them their freedom, then by his own admission he is still a SLAVE; and whatever opinions may be entertained in favor of the citizenship of a free person of the AFRICAN race, no one supposes that a SLAVE is a citizen of the State or of the United States. If, therefore, the acts done by his owner did not make them free persons, he is <u>STILL A SLAVE</u>, and certainly incapable of suing in the character of a citizen.

The principle of law is too well settled to be disputed, that a court can give no judgment for either party, where it has no jurisdiction; and if, upon the shobranch of Scott himself, it appeared that he was still a **SLAVE**, the case ought to have been dismissed, and the judgment against him and in favor of the defendant for costs, is, like that on the plea in abatement, erroneous, and the suit ought to have been dismissed by the Circuit Court for want of jurisdiction in that court.

But, before we proceed to examine this part of the case, it may be proper to notice an objection taken to the judicial authority of this court to decide it; and it has been said, that as this court has decided against the jurisdiction of the Circuit Court on the plea in abatement, it has no right to examine any question presented by the exception; and that anything it may say upon that part of the case will be extra-judicial, and mere obiter dicta.

This is a manifest mistake; there can be no doubt as to the jurisdiction of this court to revise the judgment of a Circuit Court, and to reverse it for any error apparent on the record, whether it be the error of giving judgment in a case over which it had no jurisdiction, or any other material error; and this, too, whether there is a plea in abatement or not.

The objection appears to have arisen from confounding writs of error to a State court, with writs of error to a Circuit Court of the United States. Undoubtedly, upon a writ of error to a State court, unless the record shows a case that gives jurisdiction, the case must be dismissed for want of jurisdiction in this court. And if it is dismissed on that ground, we have no right to examine and decide upon any question presented by the bill of exceptions, or any other part of the record. But writs of error to a State court, and to a Circuit Court of the United States, are regulated by different laws, and stand upon entirely different principles. And in a writ of error to a Circuit Court of the United States, the whole record is before this court for examination and decision; and if the sum in controversy is large enough to give jurisdiction, it is not only the right, but it is the judicial duty of the court, to examine the whole case as presented by the record; and if it appears upon its face that any material error or errors have been committed by the court below, it is the duty of this court to reverse the judgment, and remand the case. And certainly an error in passing a judgment upon the merits in favor of either party, in a case which it was not authorized to try, and over which it had no jurisdiction, is as grave an error as a court can commit.

The plea in abatement is not a plea to the jurisdiction of this court, but to the jurisdiction of the Circuit Court. And it appears by the record before us, that the Circuit Court committed an error, in deciding that it had jurisdiction, upon the facts in the case, admitted by the pleadings. It is the duty of the appellate tribunal to correct this error; but that could not be done by dismissing the case for want of jurisdiction here--for that would leave the erroneous judgment in full force, and the injured party without remedy. And the appellate court therefore exercises the power for which alone appellate courts are constituted, by reversing the judgment of the court below for this error. It exercises its proper and appropriate jurisdiction over the judgment and proceedings of the Circuit Court, as they appear upon the record brought up by the writ of error.

The correction of one error in the court below does not deprive the appellate court of the power of examining further into the record, and correcting any other material errors which may have been committed by the inferior court. There is certainly no rule of law--nor any practice--nor any decision of a court--which even questions this power in the appellate tribunal. On the contrary, it is the daily practice of this court, and of all appellate courts where they reverse the judgment of an inferior court for error, to correct by its opinions whatever errors may appear on the record material to the case; and they have always held it to be their duty to do so where the silence of the court might lead to misconstruction or future controversy, and the point has been relied on by either side, and argued before the court.

In the case before us, we have already decided that the Circuit Court erred in deciding that it had jurisdiction upon the facts admitted by the pleadings. And it appears that, in the further progress of the case, it acted upon the erroneous principle it had decided on the pleadings, and gave judgment for the defendant, where, upon the facts admitted in the exception, it had no jurisdiction. We are at a loss to understand upon what principle of law, applicable to appellate jurisdiction, it can be supposed that this court has not judicial authority to correct the last-mentioned error, because they had before corrected the former; or by what process of reasoning it can be made out, that the error of an inferior court in actually pronouncing judgment for one of the parties, in a case in which it had no jurisdiction, cannot be looked into or corrected by this court, because we have decided a similar question presented in the pleadings. The last point is distinctly presented by the facts contained in the plaintiff's own bill of exceptions, which he himself brings here by this writ of error. It was the point which chiefly occupied the attention of the counsel on both sides in the argument--and the judgment which this court must render upon both errors is precisely the same. It must, in each of them, exercise jurisdiction over the judgment, and reverse it for the errors committed by the court below; and issue a mandate to the Circuit Court to conform its judgment to the opinion pronounced by this court, by dismissing the case for want of jurisdiction in the Circuit Court. This is the constant and invariable practice of this court, where it reverses a judgment for want of jurisdiction in the Circuit Court. . . .

The case before us still more strongly imposes upon this court the duty of examining whether the court below has not committed an error, in taking jurisdiction and giving a judgment for costs in favor of the defendant; . . . in this case it does appear that the plaintiff was born a SLAVE; and if the facts upon which he relies have not made him free, then it appears affirmatively on the record that he is not a citizen, and consequently his suit against Sandford was not a suit between citizens of different States, and the court had no authority to pass any judgment between the parties. The suit ought, in this view of it, to have been dismissed by the Circuit Court, and its judgment in favor of Sandford is erroneous, and must be reversed.

It is true that the result either way, by dismissal or by a judgment for the defendant, makes very little, if any, difference in a pecuniary or personal point of view to either party. But the fact that the result would be very nearly the same to the parties in either form of judgment, would not justify this court in sanctioning an error in the judgment which is patent on the record, and which, if sanctioned, might be drawn into precedent, and lead to serious mischief and injustice in some future suit.

We proceed, therefore, to inquire whether the facts relied on by the plaintiff entitled him to his freedom.

The case, as he himself states it, on the record brought here by his writ of error, is this:

The plaintiff was [an **AFRICAN**] **SLAVE**, belonging to Dr. Emerson, who was a surgeon in the army of the United States. In the year 1834, he took the plaintiff from the State of Missouri to the military post at Rock Island, in the State of Illinois, and held him there as a **SLAVE** until the month of April or May, 1836. At the time last mentioned, said Dr. Emerson removed the plaintiff from said military post at Rock Island to the military post at Fort Snelling, situate on the west bank of the Mississippi river, in the Territory known as Upper Louisiana, acquired by the United States of France, and situate north of the latitude of thirty-six degrees thirty minutes north, and north of the State of Missouri. Said Dr. Emerson held the plaintiff in **SLAVERY** at said Fort Snelling, from said last-mentioned date until the year 1838.

In the year 1835, Harriet, who is named in the second count of the plaintiff's declaration, was the **[AFRICAN] SLAVE** of Major Taliaferro, who belonged to the army of the United States. In that year, 1835, said Major Taliaferro took said Harriet to said Fort Snelling, a military post, situated as here in before stated, and kept her there as a **SLAVE** until the year 1836, and then sold and delivered her as a **SLAVE**, at said Fort Snelling, unto the said Dr. Emerson hereinbefore named. Said Dr. Emerson held said Harriet in **SLAVERY** at said Fort Snelling until the year 1838.

In the year 1836, the plaintiff and Harriet intermarried, at Fort Snelling, with the consent of Dr. Emerson, who then claimed to be their master and owner. Eliza and Lizzie, named in the third count of the plaintiff's declaration, are the fruit of that marriage. Eliza is about fourteen years old, and was born on board the steamboat Gipsey, north of the north line of the State of Missouri, and upon the river Mississippi. Lizzie is about seven years old, and was born in the State of Missouri, at the military post called Jefferson Barracks.

In the year 1838, said Dr. Emerson removed the plaintiff and said Harriet, and their said daughter Eliza, from said Fort Snelling to the State of Missouri, where they have ever since resided.

Before the commencement of this suit, said Dr. Emerson sold and conveyed the plaintiff, and Harriet, Eliza, and Lizzie, to the defendant, as **SLAVES**, and the defendant has ever since claimed to hold them, and each of them, as **SLAVES**.

In considering this part of the controversy, two questions arise: 1. Was he, together with his family, free in Missouri by reason of the stay in the territory of the United States hereinbefore mentioned? And 2. If they were not, is Scott himself free by reason of his removal to Rock Island, in the State of Illinois, as stated in the above admissions?
We proceed to examine the first question.
The act of Congress, upon which the plaintiff relies, declares that **SLAVERY** and involuntary servitude, except as a punishment for crime, shall be forever prohibited in all that part of the territory ceded by France, under the name of Louisiana, which lies north of thirty-six degrees thirty minutes north latitude, and not included within the limits of Missouri. And the difficulty which meets us at the threshold of this part of the inquiry is, whether Congress was authorized to pass this law under any of the powers granted to it by the Constitution; for if the authority is not given by that instrument, it is the duty of this court to declare it void and inoperative, and incapable of conferring freedom upon any one who is held as a **SLAVE** under the laws of any one of the States.
The counsel for the plaintiff has laid much stress upon that article in the Constitution which confers on Congress the power 'to dispose of and make all needful rules and regulations respecting the territory or other property belonging to the United States;' but, in the judgment of the court, that provision has no bearing on the present controversy, and the power there given, whatever it may be, is confined, and was intended to be confined, to the territory which at that time belonged to, or was claimed by, the United States, and was within their boundaries as settled by the treaty with Great Britain, and can have no

influence upon a territory afterwards acquired from a foreign Government. It was a special provision for a known and particular territory, and to meet a present emergency, and nothing more. . . .

The words 'rules and regulations' are usually employed in the Constitution in speaking of some particular specified power which it means to confer on the Government, and not, as we have seen, when granting general powers of legislation. As, for example, in the particular power to Congress 'to make rules for the government and regulation of the land and naval forces, or the particular and specific power to regulate commerce;' 'to establish an uniform rule of naturalization;' 'to coin **MONEY** and regulate the value thereof.' And to construe the words of which we are speaking as a general and unlimited grant of sovereignty over territories which the Government might afterwards acquire, is to use them in a sense and for a purpose for which they were not used in any other part of the instrument. But if confined to a particular Territory, in which a Government and laws had already been established, but which would require some alterations to adapt it to the new Government, the words are peculiarly applicable and appropriate for that purpose.

The necessity of this special provision in relation to property and the rights or property held in common by the confederated States, is illustrated by the first clause of the sixth article. This clause provides that 'all debts, contracts, and engagements entered into before the adoption of this Constitution, shall be as valid against the United States under this Government as under the Confederation.' This provision, like the one under consideration, was indispensable if the new Constitution was adopted. The new Government was not a mere change in a dynasty, or in a form of government, leaving the nation or sovereignty the same, and clothed with all the rights, and bound by all the obligations of the preceding one. But, when the present United States came into existence under the new Government, it was a new political body, a new nation, then for the first time taking its place in the family of nations. It took nothing by succession from the Confederation. It had no right, as its successor, to any property or rights of property which it had acquired, and was not liable for any of its obligations. It was evidently viewed in this light by the framers of the Constitution. And as the several States would cease to exist in their former confederated character upon the adoption of the Constitution, and could not, in that character, again assemble together, special provisions were indispensable to transfer to the new Government the property and rights which at that time they held in common; and at the same time to authorize it to lay taxes and appropriate **MONEY** to pay the common debt which they had contracted; and this power could only be given to it by special provisions in the Constitution. The clause in relation to the territory and other property of the United States provided for the first, and the clause last quoted provided for the other. They have no connection with the general powers and rights of sovereignty delegated to the new Government, and can neither enlarge nor diminish them. They were inserted to meet a present emergency, and not to regulate its powers as a Government.

Indeed, a similar provision was deemed necessary, in relation to treaties made by the Confederation; and when in the clause next succeeding the one of which we have last spoken, it is declared that treaties shall be the supreme law of the land, care is taken to include, by express words, the treaties made by the confederated

States. The language is: 'and all treaties made, or which shall be made, under the authority of the United States, shall be the supreme law of the land.'

Whether, therefore, we take the particular clause in question, by itself, or in connection with the other provisions of the Constitution, we think it clear, that it applies only to the particular territory of which we have spoken, and cannot, by any just rule of interpretation, be extended to territory which the new Government might afterwards obtain from a foreign nation. Consequently, the power which Congress may have lawfully exercised in this Territory, while it remained under a Territorial Government, and which may have been sanctioned by judicial decision, can furnish no justification and no argument to support a similar exercise of power over territory afterwards acquired by the Federal Government. We put aside, therefore, any argument, drawn from precedents, showing the extent of the power which the General Government exercised over **SLAVERY** in this Territory, as altogether inapplicable to the case before us.

This brings us to examine by what provision of the Constitution the present Federal Government, under its delegated and restricted powers, is authorized to acquire territory outside of the original limits of the United States, and what powers it may exercise therein over the person or property of a citizen of the United States, while it remains a Territory, and until it shall be admitted as one of the States of the Union.

There is certainly no power given by the Constitution to the Federal Government to establish or maintain colonies bordering on the United States or at a distance, to be ruled and governed at its own pleasure; nor to enlarge its territorial limits in any way, except by the admission of new States. That power is plainly given; and if a new State is admitted, it needs no further legislation by Congress, because the Constitution itself defines the relative rights and powers, and duties of the State, and the citizens of the State, and the Federal Government. But no power is given to acquire a Territory to be held and governed permanently in that character. . . .

[I]t may be safely assumed that citizens of the United States who migrate to a Territory belonging to the people of the United States, cannot be ruled as mere colonists, dependent upon the will of the General Government, and to be governed by any laws it may think proper to impose. The principle upon which our Governments rest, and upon which alone they continue to exist, is the union of States, sovereign and independent within their own limits in their internal and domestic concerns, and bound together as one people by a General Government, possessing certain enumerated and restricted powers, delegated to it by the people of the several States, and exercising supreme authority within the scope of the powers granted to it, throughout the dominion of the United States. A power, therefore, in the General Government to obtain and hold colonies and dependent territories, over which they might legislate without restriction, would be inconsistent with its own existence in its present form. Whatever it acquires, it acquires for the benefit of the people of the several States who created it. It is their trustee acting for them, and charged with the duty of promoting the interests of the whole people of the Union in the exercise of the powers specifically granted.

At the time when the Territory in question was obtained by cession from France, it contained no population fit to be associated together and admitted as a State; and it therefore was absolutely necessary to hold possession of it, as a Territory belonging to the United States, until it was settled and inhabited by a civilized community capable of self-government, and in a condition to be admitted on equal terms with the other States as a member of the Union. But, as we have before said, it was acquired by the General Government, as the representative and trustee of the people of the United States, and it must therefore be held in that character for their common and equal benefit; for it was the people of the several States, acting through their agent and representative, the Federal Government, who in fact acquired the Territory in question, and the Government holds it for their common use until it shall be associated with the other States as a member of the Union.

But until that time arrives, it is undoubtedly necessary that some Government should be established, in order to organize society, and to protect the inhabitants in their persons and property; and as the people of the United States could act in this matter only through the Government which represented them, and the through which they spoke and acted when the Territory was obtained, it was not only within the scope of its powers, but it was its duty to pass such laws and establish such a Government as would enable those by whose authority they acted to reap the advantages anticipated from its acquisition, and to gather there a population which would enable it to assume the position to which it was destined among the States of the Union. The power to acquire necessarily carries with it the power to preserve and apply to the purposes for which it was acquired. The form of government to be established necessarily rested in the discretion of Congress. It was their duty to establish the one that would be best suited for the protection and security of the citizens of the

United States, and other inhabitants who might be authorized to take up their abode there, and that must always depend upon the existing condition of the Territory, as to the number and character of its inhabitants, and their situation in the Territory. In some cases a Government, consisting of persons appointed by the Federal Government, would best subserve the interests of the Territory, when the inhabitants were few and scattered, and new to one another. In other instances, it would be more advisable to commit the powers of self-government to the people who had settled in the Territory, as being the most competent to determine what was best for their own interests. But some form of civil authority would be absolutely necessary to organize and preserve civilized society, and prepare it to become a State; and what is the best form must always depend on the condition of the Territory at the time, and the choice of the mode must depend upon the exercise of a discretionary power by Congress, acting within the scope of its constitutional authority, and not infringing upon the rights of person or rights of property of the citizen who might go there to reside, or for any other lawful purpose. It was acquired by the exercise of this discretion, and it must be held and governed in like manner, until it is fitted to be a State.

But the power of Congress over the person or property of a citizen can never be a mere discretionary power under our Constitution and form of Government. The powers of the Government and the rights and privileges of the citizen are regulated and plainly defined by the Constitution itself. And when the Territory becomes a part of the United States, the Federal Government enters into possession in the character impressed upon it by those who created it. It enters upon it with its powers over the citizen strictly defined, and limited by the Constitution, from which it derives its own existence, and by virtue of which alone it continues to exist and act as a Government and sovereignty. It has no power of any kind beyond it; and it cannot, when it enters a Territory of the United States, put off its character, and assume discretionary or despotic powers which the Constitution has denied to it. It cannot create for itself a new character separated from the citizens of the United States, and the duties it owes them under the provisions of the Constitution. The Territory being a part of the United States, the Government and the citizen both enter it under the authority of the Constitution, with their respective rights defined and marked out; and the Federal Government can exercise no power over his person or property, beyond what that instrument confers, nor lawfully deny any right which it has reserved.

A reference to a few of the provisions of the Constitution will illustrate this proposition.

For example, no one, we presume, will contend that Congress can make any law in a Territory respecting the establishment of religion, or the free exercise thereof, or abridging the freedom of speech or of the press, or the right of the people of the Territory peaceably to assemble, and to petition the Government for the redress of grievances.

Nor can Congress deny to the people the right to keep and bear arms, nor the right to trial by jury, nor compel any one to be a witness against himself in a criminal proceeding.

These powers, and others, in relation to rights of person, which it is not necessary here to enumerate, are, in express and positive terms, denied to the General Government; and the rights of private property have been guarded with equal care. Thus the rights of property are united with the rights of person, and placed on the same ground by the fifth amendment to the Constitution, which provides that no person shall be deprived of life, liberty, and property, without due process of law. And an act of Congress which deprives a citizen of the United States of his liberty or property, merely because he came himself or brought his property into a particular Territory of the United States, and who had committed no offence against the laws, could hardly be dignified with the name of due process of law.

So, too, it will hardly be contended that Congress could by law quarter a soldier in a house in a Territory without the consent of the owner, in time of peace; nor in time of war, but in a manner prescribed by law. Nor could they by law forfeit the property of a citizen in a Territory who was convicted of treason, for a longer period than the life of the person convicted; nor take private property for public use without just compensation.

The powers over person and property of which we speak are not only not granted to Congress, but are in express terms denied, and they are forbidden to exercise them. And this prohibition is not confined to the States, but the words are general, and extend to the whole territory over which the Constitution gives it power to legislate, including those portions of it remaining under Territorial Government, as well as that covered by States. It is a total absence of power everywhere within the dominion of the United States, and places the citizens of a Territory, so far as these rights are concerned, on the same footing with citizens of the States, and guards them as firmly and plainly against any inroads which the General Government might attempt, under the plea of implied or incidental powers. And if Congress itself cannot do this--if it is beyond the powers conferred on the

Federal Government--it will be admitted, we presume, that it could not authorize a Territorial Government to exercise them. It could confer no power on any local Government, established by its authority, to violate the provisions of the Constitution.

It seems, however, to be supposed, that there is a difference between property in a **SLAVE** and other property, and that different rules may be applied to it in expounding the Constitution of the United States. And the laws and usages of nations, and the writings of eminent jurists upon the relation of master and **SLAVE** and their mutual rights and duties, and the powers which Governments may exercise over it, have been dwelt upon in the argument.

But in considering the question before us, it must be borne in mind that there is no law of nations standing between the people of the United States and their Government, and interfering with their relation to each other. The powers of the Government, and the rights of the citizen under it, are positive and practical regulations plainly written down. The people of the United States have delegated to it certain enumerated powers, and forbidden it to exercise others. It has no power over the person or property of a citizen but what the citizens of the United States have granted. And no laws or usages of other nations, or reasoning of statesmen or jurists upon the relations of master and **SLAVE**, can enlarge the powers of the Government, or take from the citizens the rights they have reserved. And if the Constitution recognises the right of property of the master in a **SLAVE**, and makes no distinction between that description of property and other property owned by a citizen, no tribunal, acting under the authority of the United States, whether it be legislative, executive, or judicial, has a right to draw such a distinction, or deny to it the benefit of the provisions and guarantees which have been provided for the protection of private property against the encroachments of the Government.

Now, as we have already said in an earlier part of this opinion, upon a different point, the right of property in a **SLAVE** is distinctly and expressly affirmed in the Constitution. The right to traffic in it, like an ordinary article of merchandise and property, was guarantied to the citizens of the United States, in every State that might desire it, for twenty years. And the Government in express terms is pledged to protect it in all future time, if the **SLAVE** escapes from his owner. This is done in plain words--too plain to be misunderstood. And no word can be found in the Constitution which gives Congress a greater power over **SLAVE** property, or which entitles property of that kind to less protection that property of any other description. The only power conferred is the power coupled with the duty of guarding and protecting the owner in his rights.

Upon these considerations, it is the opinion of the court that the act of Congress which prohibited a citizen from holding and owning property of this kind in the territory of the United States north of the line therein mentioned, is not warranted by the Constitution, and is therefore void; and that neither Dred Scott himself, nor any of his family, were made free by being carried into this territory; even if they had been carried there by the owner, with the intention of becoming a permanent resident.

We have so far examined the case, as it stands under the Constitution of the United States, and the powers thereby delegated to the Federal Government.

But there is another point in the case which depends on State power and State law. And it is contended, on the part of the plaintiff, that he is made free by being taken to Rock Island, in the State of Illinois, independently of his residence in the territory of the United States; and being so made free, he was not again reduced to a state of **SLAVERY** by being brought back to Missouri.

Our notice of this part of the case will be very brief; for the principle on which it depends was decided in this court, upon much consideration, in the case of Strader et al. v. Graham, reported in 10th Howard, 82. In that case, the **SLAVES** had been taken from Kentucky to Ohio, with the consent of the owner, and afterwards brought back to Kentucky. And this court held that their status or condition, as free or **SLAVE**, depended upon the laws of Kentucky, when they were brought back into that State, and not of Ohio; and that this court had no jurisdiction to revise the judgment of a State court upon its own laws. This was the point directly before the court, and the decision that this court had not jurisdiction turned upon it, as will be seen by the report of the case.

So in this case. As Scott was a **SLAVE** when taken into the State of Illinois by his owner, and was there held as such, and brought back in that character, his status, as free or **SLAVE**, depended on the laws of Missouri, and not of Illinois.

It has, however, been urged in the argument, that by the laws of Missouri he was free on his return, and that this case, therefore, cannot be governed by the case of Strader et al. v. Graham, where it appeared, by the laws of Kentucky, that the plaintiffs continued to be **SLAVES** on their return from Ohio. But whatever doubts or opinions may, at one time, have been entertained upon this subject, we are satisfied, upon a careful examination of all the cases decided in the State courts of

Missouri referred to, that it is now firmly settled by the decisions of the highest court in the State, that Scott and his family upon their return were not free, but were, by the laws of Missouri, the property of the defendant; and that the Circuit Court of the United States had no jurisdiction, when, by the laws of the State, the plaintiff was a **SLAVE**, and not a citizen.

Moreover, the plaintiff, it appears, brought a similar action against the defendant in the State court of Missouri, claiming the freedom of himself and his family upon the same grounds and the same evidence upon which he relies in the case before the court. The case was carried before the Supreme Court of the State; was fully argued there; and that court decided that neither the plaintiff nor his family were entitled to freedom, and were still the **SLAVES** of the defendant; and reversed the judgment of the inferior State court, which had given a different decision. If the plaintiff supposed that this judgment of the Supreme Court of the State was erroneous, and that this court had jurisdiction to revise and reverse it, the only mode by which he could legally bring it before this court was by writ of error directed to the Supreme Court of the State, requiring it to transmit the record to this court. If this had been done, it is too plain for argument that the writ must have been dismissed for want of jurisdiction in this court. The case of Strader and others v. Graham is directly in point; and, indeed, independent of any decision, the language of the 25th section of the act of 1789 is too clear and precise to admit of controversy.

But the plaintiff did not pursue the mode prescribed by law for bringing the judgment of a State court before this court for revision, but suffered the case to be remanded to the inferior State court, where it is still continued, and is, by agreement of parties, to await the judgment of this court on the point. All of this appears on the record before us, and by the printed report of the case.

And while the case is yet open and pending in the inferior State court, the plaintiff goes into the Circuit Court of the United States, upon the same case and the same evidence, and against the same party, and proceeds to judgment, and then brings here the same case from the Circuit Court, which the law would not have permitted him to bring directly from the State court. And if this court takes jurisdiction in this form, the result, so far as the rights of the respective parties are concerned, is in every respect substantially the same as if it had in open violation of law entertained jurisdiction over the judgment of the State court upon a writ of error, and revised and reversed its judgment upon the ground that its opinion upon the question of law was erroneous. It would ill become this court to sanction such an attempt to evade the law, or to exercise an appellate power in this circuitous way, which it is forbidden to exercise in the direct and regular and invariable forms of judicial proceedings.

Upon the whole, therefore, it is the judgment of this court, that it appears by the record before us that the plaintiff in error is not a citizen of Missouri, in the sense in which that word is used in the Constitution; and that the Circuit Court of the United States, for that reason, had no jurisdiction in the case, and could give no judgment in it. Its judgment for the defendant must, consequently, be reversed, and a mandate issued, directing the suit to be dismissed for want of jurisdiction.

Mr. Justice WAYNE.

Concurring as I do entirely in the opinion of the court, as it has been written and read by the Chief Justice--without any qualification of its reasoning or its conclusions--I shall neither read nor file an opinion of my own in this case, which I prepared when I supposed it might be necessary and proper for me to do so.

. . .

Two of the judges, Mr. Justices McLean and Curtis, dissent from the opinion of the court. A third, Mr. Justice Nelson, gives a separate opinion upon a single point in the case, with which I concur, assuming that the Circuit Court had jurisdiction; but he abstains altogether from expressing any opinion upon the eighth section of the act of 1820, known commonly as the Missouri Compromise law, and six of us declare that it was unconstitutional.

I have already said that the opinion of the court has my unqualified assent.

Mr. Justice NELSON.

. . . I have arrived at the conclusion, that the judgment of the court below should be affirmed.

Mr. Justice GRIER.

I concur in the opinion delivered by Mr. Justice Nelson on the questions discussed by him.

I also concur with the opinion of the court as delivered by the Chief Justice, that the act of Congress of 6th March, 1820, is unconstitutional and void; and that, assuming the facts as stated in the opinion, the plaintiff cannot sue as a citizen of Missouri in the courts of the United States. . . .

Mr. Justice DANIEL concurred.

Mr. Justice CAMPBELL.

I concur in the judgment pronounced by the Chief Justice. And, in my opinion, that clause confers no power upon Congress to dissolve the relations of the master and **SLAVE** on the domain of the United States, either within or without any of the States. . . .

Mr. Justice CATRON.[concurring opinion omitted]
Mr. Justice McLEAN and Mr. Justice CURTIS dissented.
Mr. Justice CURTIS dissenting.
I dissent from the opinion pronounced by the Chief Justice, and from the judgment which the majority of the court think it proper to render in this case. . . .
. . .
The conclusions at which I have arrived on this part of the case are:
First. That the free native-born citizens of each State are citizens of the United States.
Second. That as free colored persons born within some of the States are citizens of those States, such persons are also citizens of the United States.
Third. That every such citizen, residing in any State, has the right to sue and is liable to be sued in the Federal courts, as a citizen of that State in which he resides.
Fourth. That as the plea to the jurisdiction in this case shows no facts, except that the plaintiff was of **AFRICAN** descent, and his ancestors were sold as **SLAVES**, and as these facts are not inconsistent with his citizenship of the United States, and his residence in the State of Missouri, the plea to the jurisdiction was bad, and the judgment of the Circuit Court overruling it was correct.
I dissent, therefore, from that part of the opinion of the majority of the court, in which it is held that a person of **AFRICAN** descent cannot be a citizen of the United States; and I regret I

must go further, and dissent both from what I deem their assumption of authority to examine the constitutionality of the act of Congress commonly called the Missouri compromise act, and the grounds and conclusions announced in their opinion.

Having first decided that they were bound to consider the sufficiency of the plea to the jurisdiction of the Circuit Court, and having decided that this plea showed that the Circuit Court had not jurisdiction, and consequently that this is a case to which the judicial power of the United States does not extend, they have gone on to examine the merits of the case as they appeared on the trial before the court and jury, on the issues joined on the pleas in bar, and so have reached the question of the power of Congress to pass the act of 1820. On so grave a subject as this, I feel obliged to say that, in my opinion, such an exertion of judicial power transcends the limits of the authority of the court, as described by its repeated decisions, and, as I understand, acknowledged in this opinion of the majority of the court.

For these reasons, I am of opinion that so much of the several acts of Congress as prohibited **SLAVERY** and involuntary servitude within that part of the Territory of Wisconsin lying north of thirty-six degrees thirty minutes north latitude, and west of the river Mississippi, were constitutional and valid laws. . .

In my opinion, the judgment of the Circuit Court should be reversed, and the cause remanded for a new trial.

Abraham Lincoln
1809-1865

16th President of the United States

Abraham Lincoln On The Dred Scott Decision (1857)

The myth of Abraham Lincoln's (1809-1865) love for **AFRICAN** freedom and hatred for injustice is steeped in American folklore. He was born in Kentucky, a **SLAVE** state. He spent some time in Indiana and eventually moved to Illinois. He adopted Illinois as his home state. The political base he created in Illinois would one day support his successful drive to the White House in 1860.

He and his family were considered "Trash" by "socially respectable" Whites of his day. He was lacking in formal education, but bristling with ambition. He was an attorney by profession. He served as an Illinois state legislator and United States Congressman from Illinois briefly.

He was called the "Great Emancipator." He was also called "Honest Abe." The truth is, he was neither. He was perhaps one of the greatest political **FRAUDS** produced by the 19th Century American political context.[1] He despised persons of **AFRICAN** descent! He even advocated that free **AFRICANS** be deported. This is ironic! There is strong evidence that he was of **AFRICAN** desent![2]

---

[1] Lerone Bennett, Jr. provides us with exhaustive evidence to support my statement in his well-researched volume entitled, *Forced Into Glory: Abraham Lincoln's White Dream*, (Chicago: Johnson Publishing company, 2000).

[2] After a careful reading of historical documents and anecdotes at his disposal, J.A. Rogers provided a strong case for Lincoln's **AFRICAN** ancestry.

Lincoln's reflection on the Dred Scott decision are part of a series of debates held during the US Senate race in Illinois as he campaigned against the incumbent, and Democrat, Stephen Douglas. He lost to Douglas. He would face Douglas again in the 1860 race for the presidency. That time, he won.

Lincoln did, however, have a passionate desire to preserve the Federal Union. He was an unbending advocate for the preservation of America's Constitutional form of government.

In his response to the Dred Scott decision, Lincoln displays a bit of ambiguity in his thoughts towards the question of **AFRICAN** existence in America. He couches his response to the decision in superfluous verbiage related to questions pertaining to states rights and the then hot topic of Mormon polygamous marital practices in Utah. I highlighted all of Lincoln's comments concerning Scott and his feelings concerning **AFRICANS** by using a ***bold/italic*** format. What the highlights will show is that he, if not a **SLAVEHOLDER,** was wholly indifferent to the plight of the **AFRICAN**, both **SLAVE** and "**FREE**." He viewed them as nuisances to be disposed of!

Evidence suggests that Lincoln was the illegitimate son of an **AFRICAN** that had engaged in sexual relations with his mother, Nancy Hanks. J.A. Rogers, *The Five Negro Presidents*, (Saint Petersburg, FL: Helga M. Rogers, 1993), 8-9. In the same book, Rogers claimed that there were four more American Presidents that were identifiably "White," but were in actuality **AFRICAN**. Ever so careful the historian, he named three more, but declined to reveal the identity of the fifth due to a lack of credible source material. The ones he would identify were as follows, Thomas Jefferson, Andrew Jackson, and Warren G. Harding, Ibid. 6-13. Other prominent Americans named in his study were Lincoln's first Vice President, Hannibal Hamlin, and Alexander Hamilton.

Lincoln's ability to weave disparate issues in such a way as to *say much and at the same time say nothing* would propel him to the White House three years later and make him America's sixteenth president.

It would also assist in propelling the nation to Civil War.

Abraham Lincoln On The Dred Scott Decision (1857)

June 26, 1857

FELLOW CITIZENS:—I am here to-night, partly by the invitation of some of you, and partly by my own inclination. *Two weeks ago Judge Douglas spoke here on the several subjects of Kansas, the Dred Scott decision, and Utah.* I listened to the speech at the time, and have read the report of it since. It was intended to controvert opinions which I think just, and to assail (politically, not personally,) those men who, in common with me, entertain those opinions. For this reason I wished then, and still wish, to make some answer to it, which I now take the opportunity of doing.

I begin with Utah. If it prove to be true, as is probable, that the people of Utah are in open rebellion to the United States, then Judge Douglas is in favor of repealing their territorial organization, and attaching them to the adjoining States for judicial purposes. I say, too, if they are in rebellion, they ought to be somehow coerced to obedience; and I am not now prepared to admit or deny that the Judge's mode of coercing them is not as good as any. The Republicans can fall in with it without taking back anything they have ever said. To be sure, it would be a considerable backing down by Judge Douglas from his much vaunted doctrine of self-government for the territories; but this is only additional proof of what was very plain from the beginning, that that doctrine was a mere deceitful pretense for the benefit of **SLAVERY**. Those who could not see that much in the Nebraska act itself, which forced Governors, and Secretaries, and Judges on the people of the territories, without their choice or consent, could not be made to see, though one should rise from the dead to testify.

But in all this, it is very plain the Judge evades the only question the Republicans have ever pressed upon the Democracy in regard to Utah. That question the Judge well knows to be this: "If the people of Utah shall peacefully form a State Constitution tolerating polygamy, will the Democracy admit them into the Union?" There is nothing in the **United States Constitution** or law against polygamy; and why is it not a part of the Judge's "sacred right of self-government" for that people to have it, or rather to keep it, if they choose? These questions, so far as I know, the Judge never answers. It might involve the Democracy to answer them either way, and they go unanswered.

As to Kansas. The substance of the Judge's speech on Kansas is an effort to put the free State men in the wrong for not voting at the election of delegates to the Constitutional Convention. He says: "There is every reason to hope and believe that the law will be fairly interpreted and impartially executed, so as to insure to every bona fide inhabitant the free and quiet exercise of the elective franchise."

It appears extraordinary that Judge Douglas should make such a statement. He knows that, by the law, no one can vote who has not been registered; and he knows that the free State men place their refusal to vote on the ground that but few of them have been registered. It is possible this is not true, but Judge Douglas knows it is asserted to be true in letters, newspapers and public speeches, and borne by every mail, and blown by every breeze to the eyes and ears of the world. He knows it is boldly declared that the people of many whole counties, and many whole neighborhoods in others, are left unregistered; yet, he does not venture to contradict the declaration, nor to point out how they can vote without being registered; but he just slips along, not seeming to know there is any such question of fact, and complacently declares: "There is every reason to hope and believe that the law will be fairly and impartially executed, so as to insure to every bona fide inhabitant the free and quiet exercise of the elective franchise."

I readily agree that if all had a chance to vote, they ought to have voted. If, on the contrary, as they allege, and Judge Douglas ventures not to particularly contradict, few only of the free State men had a chance to vote, they were perfectly right in staying from the polls in a body.

By the way since the Judge spoke, the Kansas election has come off. The Judge expressed his confidence that all the Democrats in Kansas would do their duty-including "free state Democrats" of course. The returns received here as yet are very incomplete; but so far as they go, they indicate that only about one sixth of the registered voters, have really voted; and this too, when not more, perhaps, than one half of the rightful voters have been registered, thus showing the thing to have been altogether the most exquisite farce ever enacted. I am watching with considerable interest, to ascertain what figure "the free state Democrats" cut in the concern. Of course they voted—all democrats do their duty—and of course they did not vote for **SLAVE**-state candidates. We soon shall know how many delegates they elected, how many candidates they had, pledged for a free state; and how many votes were cast for them.

Allow me to barely whisper my suspicion that there were no such things in Kansas "as free state Democrats"—that they were altogether mythical, good only to figure in newspapers and speeches in the free states. If there should prove to be one real living free state Democrat in Kansas, I suggest that it might be well to catch him, and stuff and preserve his skin, as an interesting specimen of that soon to be extinct variety of the genus, Democrat.

And now as to the Dred Scott decision. That decision declares two propositions—first, that [an **AFRICAN**] cannot sue in the U.S. Courts; and secondly, that Congress cannot prohibit **SLAVERY** in the Territories. It was made by a divided court—dividing differently on the different points. Judge Douglas does not discuss the merits of the decision; and, in that respect, I shall follow his example, believing I could no more improve on McLean and Curtis, than he could on Taney.

He denounces all who question the correctness of that decision, as offering violent resistance to it. But who resists it? *Who has, in spite of the decision, declared Dred Scott free, and resisted the authority of his master over him?*

Judicial decisions have two uses—first, to absolutely determine the case decided, and secondly, to indicate to the public how other similar cases will be decided when they arise.&nabp; For the latter use, they are called "precedents" and "authorities."

We believe, as much as Judge Douglas, (perhaps more) in obedience to, and respect for the judicial department of government. We think its decisions on Constitutional questions, when fully settled, should control, not only the particular cases decided, but the general policy of the country, subject to be disturbed only by amendments of the Constitution as provided in that instrument itself. More than this would be revolution. ***But we think the Dred Scott decision is erroneous.*** We know the court that made it, has often over-ruled its own decisions, and we shall do what we can to have it to over-rule this. We offer no resistance to it.

Judicial decisions are of greater or less authority as precedents, according to circumstances. That this should be so, accords both with common sense, and the customary understanding of the legal profession.

If this important decision had been made by the unanimous concurrence of the judges, and without any apparent partisan bias, and in accordance with legal public expectation, and with the steady practice of the departments throughout our history, and had been in no part, based on assumed historical facts which are not really true; or, if wanting in some of these, it had been before the court more than once, and had there been affirmed and re-affirmed through a course of years, it then might be, perhaps would be, factious, nay, even revolutionary, to not acquiesce in it as a precedent.

But when, as it is true we find it wanting in all these claims to the public confidence, it is not resistance, it is not factious, it is not even disrespectful, to treat it as not having yet quite established a settled doctrine for the country—But **Judge Douglas considers this view awful. Hear him:**
"The courts are the tribunals prescribed by the Constitution and created by the authority of the people to determine, expound and enforce the law. Hence, whoever resists the final decision of the highest judicial tribunal, aims a deadly blow to our whole Republican system of government—a blow, which if successful would place all our rights and liberties at the mercy of passion, anarchy and violence. I repeat, therefore, that if resistance to the decisions of the Supreme Court of the United States, in a matter like the points decided in the Dred Scott case, clearly within their jurisdiction as defined by the Constitution, shall be forced upon the country as a political issue, it will become a distinct and naked issue between the friends and the enemies of the Constitution—the friends and the enemies of the supremacy of the laws."

Why this same Supreme court once decided a national bank to be constitutional; but Gen. Jackson, as **President of the United States**, disregarded the decision, and vetoed a bill for a re-charter, partly on constitutional ground, declaring that each public functionary must support the Constitution, "as he understands it." But hear the General's own words. Here they are, taken from his veto message:
"It is maintained by the advocates of the bank, that its constitutionality, in all its features, ought to be considered as settled by precedent, and by the decision of the Supreme Court.

To this conclusion I cannot assent. Mere precedent is a dangerous source of authority, and should not be regarded as deciding questions of constitutional power, except where the acquiescence of the people and the States can be considered as well settled. So far from this being the case on this subject, an argument against the bank might be based on precedent. One Congress in 1791, decided in favor of a bank; another in 1811, decided against it. One Congress in 1815 decided against a bank; another in 1816 decided in its favor. Prior to the present congress, therefore the precedents drawn from that source were equal. If we resort to the States, the expressions of legislative, judicial and executive opinions against the bank have been probably to those in its favor as four to one. There is nothing in precedent, therefore, which if its authority were admitted, ought to weigh in favor of the act before me. "

I drop the quotations merely to remark that all there ever was, in the way of precedent up to the Dred Scott decision, on the points therein decided, had been against that decision. But hear Gen. Jackson further—

"If the opinion of the Supreme court covered the whole ground of this act, it ought not to control the co-ordinate authorities of this Government. The Congress, the executive and the court, must each for itself be guided by its own opinion of the Constitution. Each public officer, who takes an oath to support the Constitution, swears that he will support it as he understands it, and not as it is understood by others. "

Again and again have I heard Judge Douglas denounce that bank decision, and applaud Gen. Jackson for disregarding it. It would be interesting for him to look over his recent speech, and see how exactly his fierce philippics against us for resisting Supreme Court decisions, fall upon his own head. It will call to his mind a long and fierce political war in this country, upon an issue which, in his own language, and, of course, in his own changeless estimation, was "a distinct and naked issue between the friends and the enemies of the Constitution," and in which war he fought in the ranks of the enemies of the Constitution.

I have said, in substance, that the Dred Scott decision was, in part, based on assumed historical facts which were not really true; and I ought not to leave the subject without giving some reasons for saying this; I therefore give an instance or two, which I think fully sustain me. Chief Justice Taney, in delivering the opinion of the majority of the Court, insists at great length that [AFRICANS] were no part of the people who made, or for whom was made, the Declaration of Independence, or the Constitution of the United States.

On the contrary, Judge Curtis, in his dissenting opinion, shows that in five of the then thirteen states, to wit, New Hampshire, Massachusetts, New York, New Jersey and North Carolina, free **[AFRICANS]** were voters, and, in proportion to their numbers, had the same part in making the Constitution that the White people had. He shows this with so much particularity as to leave no doubt of its truth; and, as a sort of conclusion on that point, holds the following language:

"The Constitution was ordained and established by the people of the United States, through the action, in each State, of those persons who were qualified by its laws to act thereon in behalf of themselves and all other citizens of the State. In some of the States, as we have seen, colored persons were among those qualified by law to act on the subject. These colored persons were not only included in the body of 'the people of the United States,' by whom the Constitution was ordained and established; but in at least five of the States they had the power to act, and, doubtless, did act, by their suffrages, upon the question of its adoption."

Again, Chief Justice Taney says: "It is difficult, at this day to realize the state of public opinion in relation to that unfortunate race, which prevailed in the civilized and enlightened portions of the world at the time of the Declaration of Independence, and when the Constitution of the United States was framed and adopted." And again, after quoting from the Declaration, he says: "The general words above quoted would seem to include the whole human family, and if they were used in a similar instrument at this day, would be so understood."

In these the Chief Justice does not directly assert, but plainly assumes, as a fact, that the public estimate of the black man is more favorable now than it was in the days of the Revolution. This assumption is a mistake. In some trifling particulars, the condition of that race has been ameliorated; but, as a whole, in this country, the change between then and now is decidedly the other way; and their ultimate destiny has never appeared so hopeless as in the last three or four years. In two of the five States—New Jersey and North Carolina—that then gave the free **[AFRICAN]** the right of voting, the right has since been taken away; and in a third—New York—it has been greatly abridged; while it has not been extended, so far as I know, to a single additional State, though the number of the States has more than doubled. In those days, as I understand, masters could, at their own pleasure, emancipate their **SLAVES**; but since then, such legal restraints have been made upon emancipation, as to amount almost to prohibition. In those days, Legislatures held the unquestioned power to abolish **SLAVERY**, in their respective States; but now it is becoming quite fashionable for State Constitutions to withhold that power from the Legislatures. In those days, by common consent, the spread of the black man's bondage to new countries was prohibited; but now, Congress decides that it will not continue the prohibition, and the Supreme Court decides that it could not if it would. In those days, our Declaration of Independence was held sacred by all, and thought to include all; but now, to aid in making the bondage of the [AFRICAN] universal and eternal, it is assailed, and sneered at, and construed, and hawked at, and torn, till, if its framers could rise from their graves, they could not at all recognize it. All the powers of earth seem rapidly combining against him. Mammon is after him; ambition follows, and philosophy follows, and the Theology of the day is fast joining the cry. They have him in his prison house; they have searched his person, and left no prying instrument with him. One after another they have closed the heavy iron doors upon him, and now they have him, as it were, bolted in with a lock of a hundred keys, which can never be unlocked without the concurrent of every key; the keys in the hands of a hundred different men, and they scattered to a hundred different and distant places; and they stand musing as to what invention, in all the dominions of mind and matter, can be produced to make the impossibility of his escape more complete than it is.

It is grossly incorrect to say or assume, that the public estimate of the [AFRICAN] is more favorable now than it was at the origin of the government.

Three years and a half ago, Judge Douglas brought forward his famous Nebraska bill. The country was at once in a blaze. He scorned all opposition, and carried it through Congress. Since then he has seen himself superseded in a Presidential nomination, by one indorsing the general doctrine of his measure, but at the same time standing clear of the odium of its untimely agitation, and its gross breach of national faith; and he has seen that successful rival Constitutionally elected, not by the strength of friends, but by the division of adversaries, being in a popular minority of nearly four hundred thousand votes. He has seen his chief aids in his own State, Shields and Richardson, politically speaking, successively tried, convicted, and executed, for an offense not their own, but his. And now he sees his own case, standing next on the docket for trial.

There is a natural disgust in the minds of nearly all White people, to the idea of an indiscriminate amalgamation of the White and black races; and Judge Douglas evidently is basing his chief hope, upon the chances of being able to appropriate the benefit of this disgust to himself. If he can, by much drumming and repeating, fasten the odium of that idea upon his adversaries, he thinks he can struggle through the storm. He therefore clings to this hope, as a drowning man to the last plank. *He makes an occasion for lugging it in from the opposition to the Dred Scott decision.* He finds the Republicans insisting that the Declaration of Independence includes ALL men, black as well as White; and forthwith he boldly denies that it includes [**AFRICANS**] at all, and proceeds to argue gravely that all who contend it does, do so only because they want to vote, and eat, and sleep, and marry with [**AFRICANS**]! He will have it that they cannot be consistent else. *Now I protest against that counterfeit logic which concludes that, because I do not want a black woman for a SLAVE I must necessarily want her for a wife. I need not have her for either, I can just leave her alone. In some respects she certainly is not my equal; but in her natural right to eat the bread she earns with her own hands without asking leave of any one else, she is my equal, and the equal of all others.*

Chief Justice Taney, in his opinion in the Dred Scott case, admits that the language of the Declaration is broad enough to include the whole human family, but he and Judge Douglas argue that the authors of that instrument did not intend to include [AFRICANS], by the fact that they did not at once, actually place them on an equality with the Whites. Now this grave argument comes to just nothing at all, by the other fact, that they did not at once, or ever afterwards, actually place all White people on an equality with one or another. And this is the staple argument of both the Chief Justice and the Senator, for doing this obvious violence to the plain unmistakable language of the Declaration. I think the authors of that notable instrument intended to include all men, but they did not intend to declare all men equal in all respects. They did not mean to say all were equal in color, size, intellect, moral developments, or social capacity. They defined with tolerable distinctness, in what respects they did consider all men created equal—equal in "certain inalienable rights, among which are life, liberty, and the pursuit of happiness." This they said, and this meant. They did not mean to assert the obvious untruth, that all were then actually enjoying that equality, nor yet, that they were about to confer it immediately upon them. In fact they had no power to confer such a boon. They meant simply to declare the right, so that the enforcement of it might follow as fast as circumstances should permit. They meant to set up a standard maxim for free society, which should be familiar to all, and revered by all; constantly looked to, constantly labored for, and even though never perfectly attained, constantly approximated, and thereby constantly spreading and deepening its influence, and augmenting the happiness and value of life to all people of all colors everywhere. The assertion that "all men are created equal" was of no practical use in effecting our separation from Great Britain; and it was placed in the Declaration, not for that, but for future use. Its authors meant it to be, thank God, it is now proving itself, a stumbling block to those who in after times might seek to turn a free people back into the hateful paths of despotism. They knew the proneness of prosperity to breed tyrants, and they meant when such should re-appear in this fair land and commence their vocation they should find left for them at least one hard nut to crack.

I have now briefly expressed my view of the meaning and objects of that part of the Declaration of Independence which declares that "all men are created equal."
Now let us hear Judge Douglas' view of the same subject, as I find it in the printed report of his late speech. Here it is:
"No man can vindicate the character, motives and conduct of the signers of the Declaration of Independence, except upon the

hypothesis that they referred to the White race alone, and not to the **AFRICAN**, when they declared all men to have been created equal—that they were speaking of British subjects on this continent being equal to British subjects born and residing in Great Britain—that they were entitled to the same inalienable rights, and among them were enumerated life, liberty and the pursuit of happiness. The Declaration was adopted for the purpose of justifying the colonists in the eyes of the civilized world in withdrawing their allegiance from the British crown, and dissolving their connection with the mother country. "
My good friends, read that carefully over some leisure hour, and ponder well upon it—see what a mere wreck—mangled ruin—it makes of our once glorious Declaration.

"They were speaking of British subjects on this continent being equal to British subjects born and residing in Great Britain!" Why, according to this, not only [**AFRICANS**] but White people outside of Great Britain and America are not spoken of in that instrument. The English, Irish and Scotch, along with White Americans, were included to be sure, but the French, Germans and other White people of the world are all gone to pot along with the Judge's inferior races.

I had thought the Declaration promised something better than the condition of British subjects; but no, it only meant that we should be equal to them in their own oppressed and unequal condition. According to that, it gave no promise that having kicked off the King and Lords of Great Britain, we should not at once be saddled with a King and Lords of our own.

I had thought the Declaration contemplated the progressive improvement in the condition of all men everywhere; but no, it merely "was adopted for the purpose of justifying the colonists in the eyes of the civilized world in withdrawing their allegiance from the British crown, and dissolving their connection with the mother country." Why, that object having been effected some eighty years ago, the Declaration is of no practical use now—mere rubbish—old wadding left to rot on the battlefield after the victory is won.

I understand you are preparing to celebrate the "Fourth," tomorrow week. What for? The doings of that day had no reference to the present; and quite half of you are not even descendants of those who were referred to at that day. But I suppose you will celebrate; and will even go so far as to read the Declaration. Suppose after you read it once in the old fashioned way, you read it once more with Judge Douglas' version. It will then run thus: "We hold these truths to be self-evident that all British subjects who were on this continent eighty-one years ago, were created equal to all British subjects born and then residing in Great Britain."

And now I appeal to all—to Democrats as well as others,—are you really willing that the Declaration shall be thus frittered away?—thus left no more at most, than an interesting memorial of the dead past? thus shorn of its vitality, and practical value; and left without the germ or even the suggestion of the individual rights of man in it?

But Judge Douglas is especially horrified at the thought of the mixing blood by the White and black races: agreed for once—a thousand times agreed. *There are White men enough to marry all the White women, and black men enough to marry all the black women; and so let them be married. On this point we fully agree with the Judge; and when he shall show that his policy is better adapted to prevent amalgamation than ours we shall drop ours, and adopt his. Let us see. In 1850 there were in the United States, 405,751, mulattoes. Very few of these are the offspring of Whites and free blacks; nearly all have sprung from black SLAVES and White masters. A separation of the races is the only perfect preventive of amalgamation but as all immediate separation is impossible the next best thing is to keep them apart where they are not already together. If White and black people never get together in Kansas, they will never mix blood in Kansas. That is at least one self-evident truth. A few free colored persons may get into the free States, in any event; but their number is too insignificant to amount to much in the way of mixing blood. In 1850 there were in the free states, 56,649 mulattoes; but for the most part they were not born there—they came from the SLAVE States, ready made up. In the same year the SLAVE States had 348,874 mulattoes all of home production. The proportion of free mulattoes to free blacks—the only colored classes in the free states—is much greater in the SLAVE than in the free states. It is worthy of note too, that among the free states those which make the colored man the nearest to equal the White, have, proportionally the fewest mulattoes the least of amalgamation.* In New Hampshire, the State which goes farthest towards equality between the races, there are just 184 Mulattoes while there are in Virginia—how many do you think? 79,775, being 23,126 more than in all the free States together.

These statistics show that SLAVERY is the greatest source of amalgamation; and next to it, not the elevation, but the degeneration of the free blacks. Yet Judge Douglas dreads the slightest restraints on the spread of SLAVERY, and the slightest human recognition of the [AFRICAN], as tending horribly to amalgamation.

This very Dred Scott case affords a strong test as to which party most favors amalgamation, the Republicans or the dear union-saving Democracy. Dred Scott, his wife and two daughters were all involved in the suit. We desired the court to have held that they were citizens so far at least as to entitle them to a hearing as to whether they were free or not; and then, also, that they were in fact and in law really free. Could we have had our way, the chances of these black girls, ever mixing their blood with that of White people, would have been diminished at least to the extent that it could not have been without their consent. But Judge Douglas is delighted to have them decided to be SLAVES, and not human enough to have a hearing, even if they were free, and thus left subject to the forced concubinage of their masters, and liable to become the mothers of mulattoes in spite of themselves—the very state of case that produces nine tenths of all the mulattoes—all the mixing of blood in the nation.

Of course, I state this case as an illustration only, not meaning to say or intimate that the master of Dred Scott and his family, or any more than a per centage of masters generally, are inclined to exercise this particular power which they hold over their female SLAVES.

I have said that the separation of the races is the only perfect preventive of amalgamation. I have no right to say all the members of the Republican party are in favor of this, nor to say that as a party they are in favor of it. There is nothing in their platform directly on the subject. But I can say a very large proportion of its members are for it, and that the chief plank in their platform—opposition to the spread of **SLAVERY**—is most favorable to that separation.

Such separation, if ever effected at all, must be effected by colonization; and no political party, as such, is now doing anything directly for colonization. Party operations at present only favor or retard colonization incidentally. The enterprise is a difficult one; but "when there is a will there is a way;" and what colonization needs most is a hearty will. Will springs from the two elements of moral sense and self-interest. Let us be brought to believe it is morally right, and, at the same time, favorable to, or, at least, not against, our interest, to transfer the **AFRICAN** to his native clime, and we shall find a way to do it, however great the task may be. The children of Israel, to such numbers as to include four hundred thousand fighting men, went out of Egyptian bondage in a body.

How differently the respective courses of the Democratic and Republican parties incidentally bear on the question of forming a will—a public sentiment—for colonization, is easy to see. The Republicans inculcate, with whatever of ability—they can, that the **[AFRICAN]** is a man; that his bondage is cruelly wrong, and that the field of his oppression ought not to be enlarged. The Democrats deny his manhood; deny, or dwarf to insignificance, the wrong of his bondage; so far as possible, crush all sympathy for him, and cultivate and excite hatred and disgust against him; compliment themselves as Union-savers for doing so; and call the indefinite outspreading of his bondage "a sacred right of self-government."

The plainest print cannot be read through a gold eagle; and it will be ever hard to find many men who will send a **SLAVE** to Liberia, and pay his passage while they can send him to a new country, Kansas for instance, and sell him for fifteen hundred dollars, and the rise.

The Emancipation Proclamation (1863)

The Emancipation Proclamation was a sham. Bennett[1] has gone to great lengths to expose its fraudulent intent. The Emancipation Proclamation, effective January 1, 1863, was issued by President Lincoln. Constitutionally speaking, he had every right to issue the document. After all, didn't he hold the Constitutionally ordained office of President? But there was a much more sinister twist to this document. The Proclamation was specifically designed to serve as a political ploy—*not* a **FREEDOM CHARTER** for the **SLAVES**. His passion was *fueled by his desire to preserve the integrity of the Constitutionally mandated Federal Union*. He was **wholly indifferent** to the plight of the **SLAVES**. He said so in a letter written to the great 19th Century Newspaper Editor, Horace Greeley. Observe,

Executive Mansion,
Washington, August 22, 1862.
Hon. Horace Greeley:
Dear Sir.
I have just read yours of the 19th. addressed to myself through the New-York Tribune. If there be in it any statements, or assumptions of fact, which I may know to be erroneous, I do not, now and here, controvert them. If there be in it any inferences which I may believe to be falsely drawn, I do not now and here, argue against them. If there be perceptable [sic] in it an impatient and dictatorial tone, I waive it in

---

[1] Lerone Bennett, Jr. *Forced Into Glory: Abraham Lincoln's White Dream*, (Chicago: Johnson Publishing company, 2000).

deference to an old friend, whose heart I have always supposed to be right.

As to the policy I "seem to be pursuing" as you say, I have not meant to leave any one in doubt. ***I would save the Union. I would save it the shortest way under the Constitution.*** The sooner the national authority can be restored; the nearer the Union will be "the Union as it was." *If there be those who would not save the Union, unless they could at the same time save **SLAVERY**, I do not agree with them. If there be those who would not save the Union unless they could at the same time destroy **SLAVERY**, I do not agree with them. **My paramount object in this struggle is to save the Union, AND IS NOT EITHER TO SAVE OR TO DESTROY SLAVERY**. If I could save the Union without freeing any **SLAVE** I would do it, and if I could save it by freeing all the **SLAVES** I would do it; and if I could save it by freeing some and leaving others alone I would also do that. **What I do about SLAVERY, and the colored race, I do because I believe it helps to save the Union;** and what I forbear, I forbear because I do not believe it would help to save the Union.* I shall do *less* whenever I shall believe what I am doing hurts the cause, and I shall do *more* whenever I shall believe doing more will help the cause. I shall try to correct errors when shown to be errors; and I shall adopt new views so fast as they shall appear to be true views. ***I have here stated my purpose according to my view of official duty; and I intend no modification of my oft-expressed personal wish that all men everywhere could be free.***
Yours,
A. Lincoln.

Lincoln was desperate! He wanted to save his beloved Union at ***any and all costs***. He was also a cagey, as well as manipulative, unscrupulous politician. Lincoln was also aware of the domestic, as well as international tightrope, he was forced to walk by prosecuting the War and not allowing the Southern States to be free of their ties to the Federal Government!

Domestically, he needed the loyalty of the so-called "Border States." These states had opted to remain loyal to the central government—*but retained the practice of* **SLAVERY**. These states were **Delaware, Maryland, Kentucky, and Missouri.**

He also needed to retain the loyalty of northern Whites, both Democrat as well as Republican-- racists that were simultaneously loyal *Union men*!

Second, though there was strong sentiment for the abolition of **SLAVERY** in Great Britain, the American South's **SLAVE POPULATION** *PRODUCED* the cotton that was ever so vital to its textile industry. Prior to Egypt[2] becoming the prime source

---

[2] Great Britain, in the midst of an economic boom caused by the Industrial Revolution, was heavily dependent upon American cotton. Southern grown cotton had been an economic staple since America's pre-independence days. This dependence didn't cease with the end of the American Revolution. The British never formally recognized the Confederate Government, though it did retain extensive economic interests in the South during the Civil War. However, the British had extensive commercial interests and natural resources around the world--hence the phrase, for *that* time, "the sun never sets upon the British Empire." During the 1860s, the British attracted the attention of the somewhat delusional Albanian born governor of Ottoman Turk ruled Egypt, Ishmael Pasha. Direct Turkish control over the region had been weakening since the 1840s. Pasha was desperate to have Egypt considered a "European" country. His childlike buffoonery played into the hands of the British, who took advantage of his rather naïve desire to ape whatever he considered European "progress." In concert with the British, he developed Egypt's cotton production capacities. This lessening of dependence upon cotton from the American South, along with a highly effective Union naval blockade, effectively, stole what thunder America's **SLAVE** produced

for England's cotton needs, the American South was vital to British industry. Britain also had a large body of soldiers stationed in Canada—directly to America's north.

France was also a problem. France, under the leadership of its mentally unstable Emperor, Louis Napoleon, had a large army stationed in Mexico. Napoleon nursed hallucinogenic dreams of recreating a French Empire in North America, by using Mexico as a stepping stone. Though he occupied Mexico with a large French force from 1860 to 1867, his position was eroding by the year. With tacit support from America's embattled Federal Government, the great Mexican statesman, Benito Juarez fought a protracted, but effective, campaign that ended in the ouster of the French and the execution of Napoleon's puppet and dupe, the Austrian "Emperor," Maximilian in 1867.

The intervention of British or French troops on the side of the South would have been a disaster! Up until the time of the Union's Army of the Potomac's somewhat indecisive "victory" at Antietam in 1862, the Southern rebel armies were consistent in a series of defeats heaped upon the demoralized, and in many cases,' cowardly lily-white Union forces. These forces were led for the most part by political "hacks," and incompetents.

---

cotton had. The British could then put off recognition of the Confederacy, utilize Egyptian cotton, and remove any pretense they had for supporting Southern claims to sovereignty. On the military front, the hesitant Union General, George B. McClellan's "victory" at Antietam in 1862 was enough to make the British rethink any plans they may have had for an invasion of the United States from their stronghold in Canada.

All *bold/italic* portions of the text show Lincoln's duplicity in terms of signing a document that in practical terms had no effect upon **ENSLAVED AFRICANS**.

Note how he declares those **SLAVES** living in states *that were in rebellion against the Union free! Such territories were effectively out of his control!* But also, he makes several *exceptions* to portions of three rebellious states, Louisiana, Arkansas, and Florida. The Emancipation Proclamation was a *desperate* move on the part of a *desperate man to save* the Union! It also shows the arrogance inherited from the "**FOUNDING FATHERS**" that made it normal for non-**AFRICANS** to decide the fate of the **AFRICAN**.

The Emancipation Proclamation (1863)

Issued By President Abraham Lincoln
"Effective Date", January 1, 1863

Whereas, on the twenty-second day of September, in the year of our Lord one thousand eight hundred and sixty-two, a proclamation was issued by the **President of the United States**, containing, among other things, the following, to wit:

"That on the first day of January, in the year of our Lord one thousand eight hundred and sixty-three, all persons held as SLAVES within any State or designated part of a State, the people whereof shall then be in rebellion against the United States, shall be then, thenceforward, and forever free; and the Executive Government of the United States, including the military and naval authority thereof, will recognize and maintain the freedom of such persons, and will do no act or acts to repress such persons, or any of them, in any efforts they may make for their actual freedom.

"That the Executive will, on the first day of January aforesaid, by proclamation, designate the *States and parts of States, if any, in which the people thereof, respectively, shall then be in rebellion against the United States*; and the fact that any State, or the people thereof, shall on that day be, in good faith, represented in the Congress of the United States by members chosen thereto at elections wherein a majority of the qualified voters of such State shall have participated, shall, in the absence of strong countervailing testimony, be deemed conclusive evidence that such State, and the people thereof, are not then in rebellion against the United States."

Now, therefore I, Abraham Lincoln, **President of the United States**, by virtue of the power in me vested as Commander-in-Chief, of the Army and Navy of the United States in time of actual armed rebellion against the authority and government of the United States, and as a fit and necessary war measure for suppressing said rebellion, do, on this first day of January, in the year of our Lord one thousand eight hundred and sixty-three, and in accordance with my purpose so to do publicly proclaimed for the full period of one hundred days, from the day first above mentioned, order and designate as the States and parts of States wherein the people thereof respectively, are this day in rebellion against the United States, the following, to wit:

Arkansas, Texas, Louisiana, (except the Parishes of St. Bernard, Plaquemines, Jefferson, St. John, St. Charles, St. James Ascension, Assumption, Terrebonne, Lafourche, St. Mary, St. Martin, and Orleans, including the City of New Orleans) Mississippi, Alabama, Florida, Georgia, South Carolina, North Carolina, and Virginia, (except the forty-eight counties designated as West Virginia, and also the counties of Berkley, Accomac, Northampton, Elizabeth City, York, Princess Ann, and Norfolk, including the cities of Norfolk and Portsmouth, and which excepted parts, are for the present, left precisely as if this proclamation were not issued.

And by virtue of the power, and for the purpose aforesaid, I do order and declare that all persons held as **SLAVES** within said designated States, and parts of States, are, and henceforward shall be free; and that the Executive government of the United States, including the military and naval authorities thereof, will recognize and maintain the freedom of said persons.

And I hereby enjoin upon the people so declared to be free to abstain from all violence, unless in necessary self-defence; and I recommend to them that, in all cases when allowed, they labor faithfully for reasonable wages.

And I further declare and make known, that such persons of suitable condition, will be received into the armed service of the United States to garrison forts, positions, stations, and other places, and to man vessels of all sorts in said service.
And upon this act, sincerely believed to be an act of justice, warranted by the Constitution, upon military necessity, I invoke the considerate judgment of mankind, and the gracious favor of Almighty God.

In witness whereof, I have hereunto set my hand and caused the seal of the United States to be affixed.

Done at the City of Washington, this first day of January, in the year of our Lord one thousand eight hundred and sixty three, and of the Independence of the United States of America the eighty-seventh.

ABRAHAM LINCOLN

By the President:

WILLIAM H. SEWARD,
Secretary of State

General William T. Sherman
1820-1891

40 Acres and A Mule (1865)

William Tecumseh Sherman (1820-1891), was a brilliant, as well as, ruthless field commander. He was a veteran commander of the Civil War's western sector, i.e., Mississippi and Tennessee. He cared nothing for **AFRICANS, SLAVE** or **"FREE."** He was a non-sentimental advocate for the complete destruction, not only of an enemy's *army*, but also of the enemy's *capacity* to wage war. If any military commander in the history of warfare believed in the policy of "scorching the earth," it was William Sherman.

He began his famous "March to the Sea" through Georgia in November of 1864. Two months prior, he inaugurated his scorched earth policy by burning the city of Atlanta to the ground. He then led his 60,000-man army, divided into two columns, separated by sixty miles, and marched 300 miles towards the Atlantic Ocean, hence the term "Sherman's March to the Sea." While on the "March" his soldiers lived off the land, as they destroyed it. They also made a concentrated, as well as successful, effort to destroy the Confederacy's agricultural base—this meant the destruction and dismemberment of plantations. His soldiers systematically destroyed all factories, bridges, rail transport facilities, and public buildings in their paths.

He had no love for **AFRICAN** people. His participation in suppression of the Southern rebellion, was not primarily to abolish **SLAVERY**, was identical to that of his Commander-in-Chief, Abraham Lincoln—preservation of the Union's national, geographical, and economic integrity. If freeing **SLAVES** would further that aim, *he would do it*. If returning the **SLAVES** that flocked to his lines, while hailing him as a Messiah, to their former **MASTERS** would further that aim, *he would do that also*. In other words, emancipation of **AFRICANS** could only be a *means* for him to destroy the Confederate Army, and never could it be his *aim*.

After meeting with a group of Baptist and Methodist **AFRICAN** clergy, he issued his famous **Special Field Order No.15**. This meeting occurred at the end of his march on January 12, 1865. This "guaranteed" thousands of acres of land seized from the retreating Confederates would then be, at his orders, distributed to the local **AFRICAN** population in 40-acre lots. Mules were also to be provided.

As stated, Sherman had no love for **AFRICANS**. His field order was at best considered a temporary measure to relieve the pressure of feeding and housing **AFRICANS** that began to flock to his army! This measure was intended to expire as soon as hostilities between the Unionists and Confederates ceased.[1] Much of this land was later "re-claimed" by resurgent former Confederates after the war ended.[2]

---

[1] Eric Foner, *Reconstruction: America's Unfinished Revolution, 1863-1877*, (Philadelphia: Harper & Row, 1988), 70-71.

[2] Ibid.

Sherman's order, as well as its "temporary" nature shows the lack of protection the **AFRICANS**, had/have! "Rights" and "privileges" are, even to this day, granted to **AFRICANS** contingent upon political whim and necessity. After the devious purpose of the "40 Acres and a Mule" is fulfilled—both acreage and animal are taken from us!

40 Acres And A Mule (1865)

Special Field Orders. No. 15 Hdqtrs. Mil, Div. Of the Mississippi. In the Field, Savannah, Ga., January 16, 1865,

I. The islands from Charleston south, the abandoned rice-fields along the rivers for thirty miles back from the sea, and the country bordering the Saint John's River, Fla., are reserved and set apart for the settlement of the [**AFRICANS**] now made free by the acts of war and the proclamation of the **President of the United States**.

II. At Beaufort, Hilton Head, Savannah, Fernandina, Saint Augustine and Jacksonville the blacks may remain in their chosen or accustomed vocations; but on the islands, and in the settlements hereafter to be established, no White person whatever, unless military officers and soldiers detailed for duty, will be permitted to reside; and the sole and exclusive management of affairs will be left to the freed people themselves, subject only to the United States military authority and the acts of Congress. By the laws of war and orders of the **President of the United States**, the [**AFRICAN**] is free, and must be dealt with as such. He cannot be subjected to conscription or forced military service, save by the written orders of the highest military authority of the Department, under such regulations as the President or Congress may prescribe; domestic servants, blacksmiths, carpenters, and other mechanics will be free to select their own work and residence, but the young and able-bodied [**AFRICANS**] must be encouraged to enlist as soldiers in the service of the United States, to contribute their share toward maintaining their own freedom and securing their rights as citizens of the United States. [**AFRICANS**] so enlisted will be organized into companies, battalions, and regiments, under the orders of the United States military authorities, and will be paid, fed, and clothed according to law. The bounties paid on enlistment may, with the consent of the recruit, go to assist his family and settlement in procuring agricultural implements, seed, tools, boats, clothing, and other articles necessary for their livelihood.

III. Whenever three respectable [**AFRICANS**], heads of families shall desire to settle on land, and shall have selected for that purpose an island or a locality clearly defined within the limits above designated, the inspector of settlements and plantations will himself, or by such subordinate officer as he may appoint, give them a license to settle such island or district, and afford them such assistance as he can to enable them to establish a peaceable agricultural settlement. The three parties named will subdivide the land, under the supervision of the inspector, among themselves and such others as may choose to settle near them, so that each family shall have a plot of not more than forty acres of tillable ground, and when it borders on some water channel with not more than 800 feet water front, in the possession of which land the military authorities will afford them protection until such time as they can protect themselves or until Congress shall regulate their title. The
quartermaster may, on the requisition of the inspector of settlements and plantations, place at the disposal of the inspector one or more of the captured steamers to ply between the

settlements and one or more of the commercial points, heretofore named in orders, to afford the settlers the opportunity to supply their necessary wants and to sell the products of their land and labor.

IV. Whenever [an **AFRICAN**] has enlisted in the military service of the United States he may locate his family in any one of the settlements at Pleasure and acquire a homestead and all other rights and privileges of a settler as though present in person. In like manner [**AFRICANS**] may settle their families and engage on board the gunboats, or in fishing, or in the navigation of the inland waters, without losing any claim to land or other advantages derived from this system. But no one, unless an actual settler as above defined, or unless absent on Government service, will be entitled to claim any right to land or property in any settlement by virtue of these orders.

V. In order to carry out this system of settlement a general officer will be detailed as inspector of settlements and plantations, whose duty it shall be to visit the settlements, to regulate their police and general management, and who will furnish personally to each head of a family, subject to the approval of the **President of the United States**, a possessory title in writing, giving as near as possible the description of boundaries, and shall adjust all claims or conflicts that may arise under the same, subject to the like approval, treating such titles altogether as possessory. The same general officer will also be charged with the enlistment and organizaton of the [**AFRICAN**] recruits and protecting their interests while absent from their settlements, and will be governed by the rules and regulations prescribed by the War Department for such purpose.

VI. Brig. Gen. R. Saxton is hereby appointed inspector of settlements and plantations and will at once enter on the performance of his duties. No change is intended or desired in the settlement now on Beaufort Island, nor will any rights to property heretofore acquired be affected thereby.

By order of Maj. Gen. W. T. Sherman:
L. M. DAYTON
Assistant Adjutant-General

The Freedman's Bureau Act of 1865

The **Freedman's Bureau**, officially known as the **Bureau of Refugees, Freedmen, and Abandoned Lands**, grew out the American Freedman's Inquiry Commission. The Commission was a creation of the War Department in 1863.

By March 1865 the Commission, by act of Congress, was replaced by the Freedman's Bureau. **The Freedman's Bureau Act of 1865** as well as its provisions/mandate is below. On December 4, 1865, an amended version of the **Act** was passed by Congress (See below), and promptly vetoed by President Andrew Johnson in February of 1866. Why did he veto the **Act**? According to Foner, Johnson refused to sign the **Act** into law because he thought it to be *un*-Constitutional and, paternalistically speaking would make the **FREEDMEN** lazy and indolent.[1]

Again, we see how the ambiguities of the Constitutional process were geared against **AFRICAN** participation in the American political process. A *White* Congress, on behalf of the **FREEDMEN**, passed the **Act**. A *White* President took it upon himself to declare the **Act**, un-Constitutional and vetoed it!

Are we not in the same predicament today? Civil Rights laws can be passed, as well as *un*-passed at the whim of Congresses and/or Presidents that may, at their pleasure, be *for* us or *against* us!

---

[1] Ibid., 68-70.

The Freedman's Bureau Act of 1865

An Act to Establish a Bureau for the Relief of Freedmen and Refugees.

Be it enacted by the Senate and House of Representatives of the United States of America in Congress assembled, That there is hereby established in the War Department, to continue during the present war of rebellion and for one year thereafter, a bureau of refugees, freedmen, and abandoned lands, to which shall be committed, as hereinafter provided, the supervision and management of all abandoned lands, and the control of all subjects relating to refugees and freedmen from rebel states, or from any district of country within the territory embraced in the operations of the army, under such rules and regulations as may be prescribed by the head of the bureau and approved by the President. The said bureau shall be under the management and control of a **COMMISSIONER** to be appointed by the President, by and with the advice and consent of the Senate, whose compensation shall be three thousand dollars per annum, and such number of clerks as may be assigned to him by the Secretary of War, not exceeding one chief clerk, two of the fourth class, two of the third class, and five of the first class. And the **COMMISSIONER** and all persons appointed under this act, shall, before entering upon their duties, take the oath of office prescribed in an act entitled "An ad to Prescribe an oath of office and for other purposes, "approved July second, eighteen hundred and sixty-two, and the **COMMISSIONER** and chief clerk shall, before entering upon their duties, give bonds to the treasurer of the United States, the former in the sum of fifty thousand dollars, and the latter in the sum of ten thousand dollars, conditioned for the faithful discharge of their duties respectively, with securities to be approved as sufficient by the Attorney General, which bonds shall be filed in the office of the first comptroller of the treasury, to be by him put in suit for the benefit of any injured party upon any breach of the conditions thereof.

Sec. 2. And be it further enacted, That the Secretary of War may direct such issues of provisions, clothing, and fuel, as he may deem needful for the immediate and temporary shelter and supply of destitute and suffering refugees and freedmen and their wives and children, under such rules and regulations as he may direct.

Sec.3. And be it further enacted, That the resident may, by and with the advice and consent of the Senate, appoint an assistant **COMMISSIONER** for each of the states declared to be in insurrection, not exceeding ten in number, who shall, under the direction of the **COMMISSIONER**, aid in the execution of the provisions of this act; and he shall give a bond to the 'treasurer of the United States, in the sum of twenty thousand dollars, in the form and manner prescribed in the first section of this act. Each of said **COMMISSIONERS** shall receive an annual salary of two thousand and five hundred dollars in full compensation for all his services. And any military officer may be detailed and assigned to duty under this act without increase of pay or allowances. The **COMMISSIONER** shall, before the commencement of each regular session of congress, make full report of his proceedings with exhibits of the state of his accounts to the President, who shall communicate the same to congress, and shall also make special reports whenever required to do so by the President or either house of congress; and the assistant **COMMISSIONERS** shall make quarterly reports of their proceedings to the **COMMISSIONER**, and also such other special reports as from time to time may be required.

Sec. 4. And be it further enacted, That the **COMMISSIONER**, under the direction of the President, shall have authority to set apart, for the use of loyal refugees and freedmen, such tracts of land within the insurrectionary states as shall have been abandoned, or to which the United States shall have acquired title by confiscation or sale, or otherwise, and to every male citizen, whether refugee or freedman, as aforesaid, there shall be assigned not more than forty acres of such land, and the person to whom it was so assigned shall be protected in the use and enjoyment of the land for the term of three years at an annual rent not exceeding six per cent upon the value of such land, as it was appraised by the state authorities in the year eighteen hundred and sixty, for the purpose of **TAXATION**, and in case no such appraisal can be found, then the rental shall be based upon the estimated value of the land in said year, to be ascertained in such manner as the **COMMISSIONER** may by regulation prescribe. At the end of said term, or at any time during said term, the occupants of any parcels so assigned may purchase the land and receive such title thereto as the United States can convey, upon paying therefor the value of the land, as ascertained and fixed for the purpose of determining the annual rent aforesaid.

Sec. 5. And be it further enacted, That all acts and parts of acts inconsistent with the provisions of this act, are hereby repealed. Approved, March 3, 1865.

THE FREEDMAN'S BUREAU ACT OF 1865

An Act to amend an act entitled "an act to establish a Bureau for the relief of Freedmen and Refugees." And for other purposes.
December 4, 1865.

Sec. 4. And be it further enacted, That the President is hereby authorized to reserve from sale or from settlement, under the homestead or preemption laws, and to set apart for the use of freedmen and loyal refugees, male or female, unoccupied public lands in Florida, Mississippi, Alabama, Louisiana, and Arkansas, not exceeding in all three millions of acres of good land; and the **COMMISSIONER**, under the direction of the President, shall cause the same from time to time to be allotted and assigned, in parcels not exceeding forty acres each, to the loyal refugees and freedmen, who shall be protected in the use and enjoyment thereof for such term of time and at such annual rent as may be agreed on between the **COMMISSIONER** and such refugees or freedmen. The rental shall be based upon a valuation of the land, to be ascertained in such manner as the **COMMISSIONER** may, under the direction of the President, by regulation prescribe. At the end of such term, or sooner, if the **COMMISSIONER** shall assent thereto, the occupants of any parcels so assigned, their heirs and assigns, may purchase the land and receive a title thereto from the United States in fee, upon paying therefor the value of the land ascertained as aforesaid.

This act was passed by Congress however, it was vetoed by President Andrew W. Johnson, on Feb 19, 1866.

Amendments 13-15 of the Constitution 1865-68

Our final entry concerns itself with comments on **Amendments 13-15** in the Constitution. All three Amendments were rapidly ratified, especially by certain southern states as the "price of admission," back into the Union after the Civil War. They were cynically ratified. This cynicism was voiced by one Southern journalist in 1875. The journalist wrote,

> The [Thirteenth], Fourteenth, and Fifteenth Amendments...may stand forever; but *we intend...to make them dead letters on the statute book.*[1]

In other words, regardless as to whether the Federal Government had passed these Amendments to the Constitution, the South, with the cowardly acquiesce of the Federal Government would never allow full participation of the **AFRICAN** in social, political, or economic life! The **AFRICAN** would exist in a **SLAVE** state in perpetuity.

In 1876, the fate of the **FREEDMEN** was sealed with the election of Republican **Rutherford B. Hayes**. Hayes' election was in doubt due alleged voting irregularities in certain southern states. In a devil's bargain, he quietly offered to withdraw Federal Troops from the South as the price of his election and

---

[1] Ibid., 590.

depriving the Democrats the Presidency. With the deal struck in 1877, Federal Troops, the only force with sufficient firepower to prevent the re-**ENSLAVEMENT** of the **FREEDMEN** were withdrawn. Without Federal bayonets to insure their **FREEDOM**, the **FREEDMEN** were put under virtual "regional arrest" and nearly re-**ENSLAVED**. **AFRICAN** life in the American South was then to be defined by lynching, terrorism in the form of the Ku Klux Klan, and the infamous Black Codes.

The sorry saga of **Amendments 13-15** is but a textbook case as to how the Constitutionally mandated White power structure can give and renege on its promises to **EQUAL PROTECTION UNDER THE LAW**. What Law? Not ours! In essence, even to this day, our rights are merely *dead letters on the statute book*.

This may seem a bit extreme, but I invite you to examine the list of states in **APPENDIX F** that voted for the Amendments, and then reversed their votes! In some cases, these Amendments were not ratified by some of the states *until well into the Twentieth Century!*

Amendments 13-15 of the Constitution 1865-68

Article XIII.

Section 1.

Neither **SLAVERY** nor involuntary servitude, except as a punishment for crime whereof the party shall have been duly convicted, shall exist within the United States, or any place subject to their jurisdiction.

Section 2.

Congress shall have power to enforce this article by appropriate legislation.

Article XIV.

Section 1.

All persons born or naturalized in the United States, and subject to the jurisdiction thereof, are citizens of the United States and of the State wherein they reside. No State shall make or enforce any law which shall abridge the privileges or immunities of citizens of the United States; nor shall any State deprive any person of life, liberty, or property, without due process of law; nor deny to any person within its jurisdiction the equal protection of the laws.

Section 2.
Representatives shall be apportioned among the several States according to their respective numbers, counting the whole number of persons in each State, excluding Indians not taxed. But when the right to vote at any election for the choice of electors for President and Vice **President of the United States**, Representatives in Congress, the Executive and Judicial officers of a State, or the members of the Legislature thereof, is denied to any of the male inhabitants of such State, being twenty-one years of age, and citizens of the United States, or in any way abridged, except for participation in rebellion, or other crime, the basis of representation therein shall be reduced in the proportion which the number of such male citizens shall bear to the whole number of male citizens twenty-one years of age in such State.

Section 3.
No person shall be a Senator or Representative in Congress, or elector of President and Vice President, or hold any office, civil or military, under the United States, or under any State, who, having previously taken an oath, as a member of Congress, or as an officer of the United States, or as a member of any State legislature, or as an executive or judicial officer of any State, to support the Constitution of the United States, shall have engaged in insurrection or rebellion against the same, or given aid or comfort to the enemies thereof. But Congress may by a vote of two-thirds of each House, remove such disability.

Section 4.
The validity of the public debt of the United States, authorized by law, including debts incurred for payment of pensions and bounties for services in suppressing insurrection or rebellion, shall not be questioned. But neither the United States nor any State shall assume or pay any debt or obligation incurred in aid of insurrection or rebellion against the United States, or any claim for the loss or emancipation of any **SLAVE**; but all such debts, obligations and claims shall be held illegal and void.
Section 5.
The Congress shall have power to enforce, by appropriate legislation, the provisions of this article.

Article XV.
Section 1.
The right of citizens of the United States to vote shall not be denied or abridged by the United States or by any State on account of race, color, or previous condition of servitude.
Section 2.
The Congress shall have power to enforce this article by appropriate legislation.

Conclusion

A friend of mine, while reviewing the manuscript for this book, joked, "man, this book's publication will land you in jail!" Sadly enough, my friend's comment had more truth to it than comedy! As an **AFRICAN** preacher, I am already suspect. I acknowledge that I have a target on the back of my head! I am a candidate for covert surveillance on the part of Federal operatives. [1]

As an **AFRICAN** preacher existing in America, I have a unique responsibility, as well as burden. Perhaps the late CME Bishop Joseph Johnson put it best when he said,

> Moving across the pages of history almost unnoticed by historians, [the **AFRICAN** preacher] is one of the most colorful and dynamic figures ever to illuminate American folklore. Armed only with the grace of God and unique qualities of the gifts of [**AFRICANESS**], this spiritual giant developed and preached the Gospel which enabled the [**AFRICAN**] masses to transcend the vicissitudes of life....Man of God by calling—but often teacher, healer, caretaker, and undertaker by necessity, it was the [**AFRICAN**] preacher who took down the

---

[1] For a detailed explanation of why I make this assertion, I invite the reader to revisit Footnote 14 in the Introduction.

mutilated bodies of [**AFRICAN**] men after the mobs had done their worst.[2]

If I am guilty, it is of the crime of taking a small collection of America's Sacred Texts and analyzing them with my own commentary. America is, as I said earlier, a **PREDASTATE**. It hypocritically labels foreign countries, beyond the scope of its control, as "sponsors of terrorism." If such countries that make up the list of "terrorist states" are true sponsors of terrorism, I have no way of verifying the accusation, then they have an able tutor in America!

Ever since the British colonists declared their independence from England in 1776, America has led the way in terror! It butchered the Native American, **ENSLAVED** the **AFRICAN**, increased its landmass by purchase, or armed seizure. In the early 1890s, American agricultural interests seized the Hawaiian Islands from the Hawaiian people deposed their Queen and declared the islands American territory. In 1898, a mere 122 years after the signing of the Declaration of Independence by the **FOUNDING FRAUDS**, America seized the Philippine Islands from the Spanish and mounted a terror campaign against Filipino nationalist that it hypocritically called, the "Philippine Insurrection!" The Filipino's only crime was to follow the example of America's **FOUNDING FRAUDS** and seek *INDEPENDENCE!*

---

[2] Bishop Joseph A. Johnson, Jr., *Proclamation Theology* (Shreveport, LA: Fourth Episcopal District Press, 1977), 39-40.

America is a fraud! It is a **PREDASTATE**! However, as Jefferson mentioned in his *Notes on the State of Virginia*, God will not allow this **FRAUD** to continue indefinitiy! As a preacher, I declare that the maggots of history will one day feed upon America's rotting corpse! I may not live to see it! But if, as our Christian faith tells us, God is not respecter of people, what makes America think that God is a respecter of nations? A fate worst than that of the former Soviet Union awaits America! When, where, and how this will occur, is beyond me! But surely, it will come! I close by urging you to read the words of Frederick Douglas. They contain a condemnation of America on the occasion of the July 4, 1854 celebration of the signing of the Declaration of Independence.

Frederick Douglas' July 4, 1854 Speech

At a time like this, scorching irony, not convincing argument, is needed. O! Had I the ability, and could I reach the nation's ear, I would, today, pour out a fiery stream of biting ridicule, blasting reproach, withering sarcasm, and stern rebuke. For it is not light that is needed, but fire; it is not the gentle shower, but thunder. We need the storm, the whirlwind, and the earthquake. The feeling of the nation must be quickened; the conscience of the nation must be roused; the propriety of the nation must be startled; the hypocrisy of the nation must be exposed: And its crimes against God and man must be proclaimed and denounced. *"What, to the American slave, is your 4th of July? I answer: a day that reveals to him, more than all the other days in the year, the gross injustice and cruelty to which he is the constant victim. To him, your celebration is a sham; your boasted liberty, an unholy license; ... your denunciations of tyrants, brass-fronted impudence.* [To the slave] your shouts of liberty and equality [are] hollow mockery; your prayers and hymns, your sermons and thanksgivings, with all your religious parade and solemnity, are, to him, mere bombast, fraud, deception, impiety and hypocrisy-- a thin veil to cover up crimes which would disgrace a nation of savages. There is not a nation on the earth guilty of practices, more shocking and bloody, than are the people of these ***United States, at this very hour.***"

**THE *END*
OR WILL IT BE
A
*BEGINNING?***

Appendices

Appendix A

James Madison's View of African Humanity

Hon. James Madison, Esq.
New Haven, Mar. 14, 1823
Sir,- The foregoing [now below] was transmitted to me from a respectable correspondent in Liverpool, deeply engaged in the abolition of the **SLAVE** trade, and the amelioration of the condition of **SLAVES**. If, sir, your leisure will allow you, and it is agreeable to you to furnish brief answers to these questions, you will, I conceive, essentially serve the cause of humanity, and gratify and oblige the Society above named, and Sir, with high consideration and esteem, your most ob't serv't,
JED'H MORSE.

Do the planters generally live on their own estates? Yes.
*Does a planter with ten or fifteen **SLAVES** employ an overlooker, or does he overlook his **SLAVES** himself?* Employs an overseer for that number of **SLAVES**, with few exceptions.
Obtain estimates of the culture of Sugar and Cotton, to show what difference it makes where the planter resides on his estate, or where he employs attorneys, overlookers, &c. -------- [no answer]
Is it a common or general practice to mortgage

SLAVE *estates?* Not uncommonly the land; sometimes the **SLAVES**; very rarely both together.

*Are sales of **SLAVE** estates very frequent under execution for debt, and what proportion of the whole may be thus sold annually?* The common law, as in England, governs the relation between land and debts; **SLAVES** are often sold under execution for debt; the proportion to the whole cannot be great within a year, and varies, of course, with the amount of debts and the urgency of creditors.

Does the Planter possess the power of selling the different branches of a family separate? Yes.

When the prices of produce, Cotton, Sugar, &c., are high, do the Planters purchase, instead of raising, their corn and other provisions? Instances are rare where the tobacco planters do not raise their own provisions.

When the prices of produce are low, do they then raise their own corn and other provisions? [see 7 above]

*Do the **negroes** fare better when the Corn, &c., is raised upon their master's estate, or when he buys it?* [see 7 above]

Do the tobacco planters in American ever buy their own Corn or other food, or do they always raise it? [see 7 above]

If they always, or mostly, raise it, can any other reason be given for the difference of the system pursued by them and that pursued by the Sugar and

Cotton planters than that the cultivation of tobacco is less profitable that that of Cotton or Sugar? The proper comparison, not between the culture of tobacco and that of sugar and cotton, but between each of these cultures and that of provisions. The tobacco planter finds it cheaper to make them a part of his crop than to buy them. The cotton and sugar planters to buy them, where this is the case, than to raise them. The term, cheaper, embraces the comparative facility and certainty of procuring the supplies.

*Do any of the Planters manufacture the packages for their produce, or the clothing for their **negroes**? and if they do, are their **negroes** better clothed than when clothing is purchased?* Generally best clothed when from the household manufactures, which are increasing.

*Where, and by whom, is the Cotton bagging of the Brazils made? is it principally made by free men or **SLAVES**?* [no answer]

*Is it the general system to employ the **negroes** in task work, or by the day?* **SLAVES** seldom employed in regular task work. They prefer it only when rewarded with the surplus time gained by their industry.

*How many hours are they generally at work in the former case? how many in the latter? Which system is generally preferred by the master? which by the **SLAVES**?* [see 14 above]

Is it common to allow them a certain portion of

*time instead of their allowance of provisions? In this case, how much is allowed? Where the **SLAVES** have the option, which do they generally choose? On which system do the **SLAVES** look the best, and acquire the most comforts?* Not the practice to substitute an allowance of time for the allowance of provisions.

*Are there many small plantations where the owners possess only a few **SLAVES**? What proportion of the whole may be supposed to be held in this way?* Very many, and increasing with the progressive subdivisions of property; the proportion cannot be stated.

*In such cases, are the **SLAVES** treated or almost considered a part of the family?* The fewer the **SLAVES**, the fewer the holders of **SLAVES**, the greater the indulgence and familiarity. In districts composing large masses of **SLAVES** there is no difference in their condition, whether held in small or large numbers beyond the difference in the dispositions of the owners, and the greater strictness of attention where the number is greater.

*Do the **SLAVES** fare the best when their situations and that of the master are brought nearest together?* [see 18 above]

*In what state are the **SLAVES** as to religion or religious instruction?* There is no general system of religious instruction. There are few spots where religious worship is not within reach, and to which they do not resort. Many are regular members of

Congregations, chiefly Baptist; and some Preachers also, though rarely able to read.

Is it common for the **SLAVES** *to be regularly married?* Not common; but instances are increasing.

If a man forms an attachment to a woman on a different or distant plantation, is it the general practice for some accommodation to take place between the owners of the man and woman, so that they may live together? The accommodation not unfrequent where the plantations are very distant. The **SLAVES** prefer wives on a different plantation, as affording occasions and pretexts for going abroad, and exempting them on holidays from a share of the little calls to which those at home are liable.

In the United States of America, the **SLAVES** *are found to increase at about the rate of 3 percent per annum. Does the same take place in other places? Give a census, if such is taken. Show what cause contributes to this increase, or what prevents it where it does not take place.* The remarkable increase of **SLAVES**, as shewn by the census, results from the comparative defect of moral and prudential restraint on the sexual connexion; and from the absence, at the same, of that counteracting licentiousness of intercourse, of which the worst examples are to be traced where the African trade, as in the West Indies, kept the number of females less than of the males.

Obtain a variety of estimates from the Planters of the cost of bringing up a child, and at what age it becomes a clear gain to its owner. The annual expense of food an raiment in rearing a child may be stated at about 8, 9, or 10 dollars; and the age at which it begins to be gainful to its owner about 9 or 10 years.

*Obtain information respecting the comparative cheapness of cultivation by **SLAVES** or by free men.* The practice here does not furnish data for a comparison of cheapness between these two modes of cultivation.

Is it common for the free blacks to labour in the field? They are sometimes hired for field labour in time of time of harvest, and on other particular occasions.

Where the labourers consist of free blacks and of White men, what are the relative prices of their labour when employed about the same work? The examples are too few to have established any such relative prices.

*What is the proportion of free blacks and **SLAVES**?* See the census.

*Is it considered that the increase in the proportion of free blacks to **SLAVES** increases or diminishes the danger of insurrection?* Rather increases.

Are the free blacks employed in the defence of the Country, and do they and the Creoles preclude the necessity of European troops? --------- [no answer]

Do the free blacks appear to consider themselves

as more closely connected with the **SLAVES** *or with the White population? and in cases of insurrection, with which have they generally taken part?* More closely with the **SLAVES**, and more likely to side with them in a case of insurrection.

What is their general character with respect to industry and order, as compared with that of the **SLAVES**? Generally idle and depraved; appearing to retain the bad qualities of the **SLAVES**, with whom they continue to associate, without acquiring any of the good ones of the Whites, from whom [they] continue separated by prejudices against their colour, and other peculiarities.

Are there any instances of emancipation in particular estates, and what is the result? There are occasional instances in the present legal condition of leaving the State.

Is there any general plan of emancipation in progress, and what? None.

What was the mode and progress of emancipation in those States in America where **SLAVERY** *has ceased to exist?* -------- [no answer]

Appendix B

NAME	STATE REPRESENTED	OCCUPATION	SIGNER of DECLARATION of INDEPENDENCE	SIGNER of UNITED STATES CONSTITUTION
John Hancock	Massachusetts	Merchant	Yes	No
Samuel Adams	Massachusetts	Politician	Yes	No
John Adams	Massachusetts	Attorney	Yes	No
Robert Treat-Paine	Massachusetts	Attorney	Yes	No
Elbridge Gerry	Massachusetts	Merchant	Yes	No
Josiah Bartlett	New Hampshire	Physician	Yes	No
William Whipple	New Hampshire	Merchant	Yes	No
Matthew Thornton	New Hampshire	Physician	Yes	No
Stephen Hopkins	Rhode Island	Judge	Yes	
William Ellery	Rhode Island	Attorney	Yes	
Roger Sherman	Connecticut	Merchant	Yes	Yes
Samuel Huntington	Connecticut	Attorney	Yes	No
William Williams	Connecticut	Soldier	Yes	No
Oliver Wolcott	Connecticut	Soldier/Politician	Yes	No
William Floyd	New York	Soldier	Yes	No
Alexander Hamilton	New York	Soldier/Politician	No	Yes
Phillip Livingston	New York	Merchant	Yes	No
Francis Lewis	New York	Merchant/Soldier	Yes	No
Lewis Morris	New York	Farmer	Yes	No
Richard Stockton	New Jersey	Attorney	Yes	No
John Witherspoon	New Jersey	Educator	Yes	No
Francis Hopkinson	New Jersey	Judge	Yes	No
John Hart	New Jersey	Farmer	Yes	No
Abraham Clark	New Jersey	Attorney	Yes	No
Robert Morris	Pennsylvania	Politician	Yes	Yes
Benjamin Rush	Pennsylvania	Physician	Yes	No
Benjamin Franklin	Pennsylvania	Scientist/Diplomat	Yes	Yes
John Morton	Pennsylvania	Judge	Yes	No
George Clymer	Pennsylvania	Attorney	Yes	Yes
James Smith	Pennsylvania	Attorney	Yes	No
George Taylor	Pennsylvania	Merchant	Yes	No
James Wilson	Pennsylvania	Politician	Yes	No
George Ross	Pennsylvania	Attorney	Yes	No

NAME	STATE REPRESENTED	OCCUPATION	SIGNER of DECLARATION of INDEPENDENCE	SIGNER of UNITED STATES CONSTITUTION
Thomas Mifflin	Pennsylvania	Soldier	No	Yes
Thomas Fitzsimmons	Pennsylvania	Politician	No	Yes
Jared Ingersoll	Pennsylvania	Judge	No	Yes
Gouverneur Morris	Pennsylvania	Attorney	No	Yes
Caesar Rodney	Delaware	Politician	Yes	No
George Read	Delaware	Politician	Yes	Yes
Thomas M'Kean	Delaware	Politician	Yes	No
Gunning Bedford	Delaware	Politician/Judge	No	Yes
John Dickerson	Delaware	Attorney	No	Yes
Richard Bassett	Delaware	Judge	No	Yes
Jacob Broom	Delaware	Attorney	No	Yes
James McHenry	Maryland	Politician	No	Yes
Samuel Chase	Maryland	Politician	Yes	No
William Paca	Maryland	Politician	Yes	No
Thomas Stone	Maryland	Farmer/Attorney	Yes	No
Charles Carrol	Maryland	Attorney	Yes	No
Daniel Carrol	Maryland	Politician	Yes	No
Dan of St. Thomas Jenifer	Maryland	Politician	No	Yes
George Whyte	Virginia	SLAVEHOLDER	Yes	No
George Washington	Virginia	SLAVEHOLDER	No	No
Thomas Jefferson	Virginia	SLAVEHOLDER	Yes	No
Richard Henry Lee	Virginia	SLAVEHOLDER	Yes	No
Benjamin Harrison	Virginia	SLAVEHOLDER	Yes	No
Thomas Nelson	Virginia	SLAVEHOLDER	Yes	No
Francis L. Lee	Virginia	SLAVEHOLDER	Yes	no
Carter Braxton	Virginia	SLAVEHOLDER	Yes	No
John Blair	Virginia	SLAVEHOLDER	No	Yes
James Madison, Jr.	Virginia	SLAVEHOLDER	No	Yes
William Hooper	North Carolina	SLAVEHOLDER	Yes	No
Joseph Hewes	North Carolina	SLAVEHOLDER	Yes	No
John Penn	North Carolina	SLAVEHOLDER	Yes	No
William Blount	North Carolina	SLAVEHOLDER	No	Yes
Richard Spaight	North Carolina	SLAVEHOLDER	No	Yes
Hugh Williamson	North Carolina	SLAVEHOLDER	No	Yes
Edward Rutledge	South Carolina	SLAVEHOLDER	Yes	No

NAME	STATE REPRESENTED	OCCUPATION	SIGNER of DECLARATION of INDEPENDENCE	SIGNER of UNITED STATES CONSTITUTION
Thomas Hayward	South Carolina	SLAVEHOLDER	Yes	No
Thomas Lynch	South Carolina	SLAVEHOLDER	Yes	No
Arthur Middlton	South Carolina	SLAVEHOLDER	Yes	No
John Rutledge	South Carolina	SLAVEHOLDER	No	Yes
Charles C. Pinckney	South Carolina	SLAVEHOLDER	No	Yes
Pierce Butler	South Carolina	SLAVEHOLDER	No	Yes
Button Gwinnett	Georgia	SLAVEHOLDER	No	Yes
Lyman Hall	Georgia	SLAVEHOLDER	No	Yes
George Walton	Georgia	SLAVEHOLDER	Yes	No
Abraham Baldwin	Georgia	SLAVEHOLDER	No	Yes
William Few	Georgia	SLAVEHOLDER	No	Yes

Appendix C

BLACK CODES
LOUISIANA, 1865

An Act to Provide For and Regulate
Labor Contracts For Agricultural Pursuit.

Sec.1. Be it enacted by the Senate and House of Representatives of the State of Louisiana in general assembly convened. That all persons employed as laborers in agricultural pursuits shall be required, during the first ten days of the month of January of each year, to make contracts for labor for the then ensuing year, or for the year next ensuing the termination of their present contracts. All contracts for labor for agricultural purposes shall be made in writing, signed by the employer, and shall be made in the presence of a Justice of the Peace and two disinterested witnesses, in whose presence the contract shall be read to the laborer, and when assented to and signed by the latter, shall be considered as binding for the time prescribed.
Sec.2. Every laborer shall have full and perfect liberty to choose his employer, but, when once chosen, he shall not be allowed to leave his place of employment until the fulfillment of his contract... and if they do so leave, without cause or permission, they shall forfeit all wages earned to the time of abandonment.
Sec.8. Be it further enacted, &c., That in case of sickness of the laborer, wages for the time lost shall be deducted, and where the sickness is feigned for purposes of idleness, and also on refusal to work according to contract, double the amount of wages shall be deducted for the time lost; and also where rations have been

furnished; and should the refusal to work continue beyond three days, the offender shall be reported to a Justice of the Peace, and shall be forced to labor on roads, levees, and other public works, without pay, until the offender consents to return to his labor.

Sec.9. Be it further enacted, & c., That, when in health, the laborer shall work ten hours during the day in summer, and nine hours during the day in winter, unless otherwise stipulated in the labor contract; he shall obey all proper orders of his employer or his agent; take proper care of mules, horses, oxen, stock; also of all agricultural implements; and employers shall have the right to make a reasonable deduction from the laborer's wages for injuries done to animals or agricultural implements committed to his care, or for bad or negligent work. Bad work shall not be allowed. Failing to obey reasonable orders, neglect of duty, and leaving home without permission will be deemed disobedience; impudence, swearing, or indecent language to or in the presence of the employer, his family, or agent, or quarreling and fighting with one another, shall be deemed disobedience. For any disobedience a fine of one dollar shall be imposed on and paid by the offender. For all lost time from work-hours, unless in case of sickness, the laborer shall be fined twenty-five cents per hour. For all absence from home without leave he will be fined at the rate of two dollars per day. Laborers will not be required to labor on the Sabbath unless by special contract. For all thefts of the laborer from the employer of agricultural products, hogs, sheep, poultry, or any other property of the employer, or willful destruction of property or injury, the laborer shall pay the employer double the amount of the value of the property stolen, destroyed, or injured, one-half to be paid to the employer and the other half to be placed in the general fund provided for in this section. No live stock shall be allowed to laborers without the permission of the employer. Laborers shall not receive visitors during work-hours. All difficulties arising between the employers and laborers, under this section, shall be settled by the former; if not satisfactory to the laborers, an appeal may be had to the nearest Justice of the Peace and two freeholders, citizens, one of said citizens to be selected by the employer and the other by the laborer; and all fines imposed and collected under this section shall he deducted from wages due, and shall be placed in a common fund, to be divided among the other laborers on the plantation, except as provided for above.

Appendix D

Apprentices And Indentured Servants (Louisiana, 1865)

Sec.1. Be it enacted, That it shall be the duty of Sheriffs, Justices of the Peace, and other Civil officers of this State, to report for each and every year, all persons under the age of eighteen years, if females, and twenty-one, if males, who are orphans, or whose parents, have not the means, or who refuse to provide for and maintain said minors; and thereupon it shall be the duty of the Clerk of the District Courts to examine whether the party or parties so reported from time to time, come within the purview and meaning of this Act, and, if so, to apprentice said minor or miners, in manner and form as prescribed by the Civil Code.

Sec.2. That persons, who have attained the age of majority, may bind themselves to services to be performed in this State, for the term of five years, on such terms as they may stipulate, as domestic servants, and to work on farms, plantations. or in manufacturing establishments, which contracts shall he valid and binding on the parties to the same.

Sec.3. That in all cases where the age of the minor can not he ascertained by record testimony, the Clerk of the District Courts Mayor and President of the Police Jury, or Justices of the Peace aforesaid, shall fix the age, according to the best evidence before them.

Appendix E

Mississippi Apprentice Law (1865)

Sec.1. It shall he the duty of all sheriffs, justices of the pence, and other civil officers of the several counties in this State, to report to the probate courts of their respective counties semi-annually, at the January and July terms of said courts, all freedmen, free **negroes**, and mulattoes, under the age of eighteen, in their respective counties, beats or districts, who are orphans. or whose parent or parents have not the means or who refuse to provide for and support said miners; and thereupon it shall be the duty of said probate court to order the clerk of said court to apprentice said miners to some competent and suitable person, on such terms as the court may direct, having a particular care to the interest of said minor: Providing, that the former owner of said miners shall have the preference when, in the opinion of the court, he or she shall be a suitable person for that purpose.

Sec. 2. The said court shall be fully satisfied that the person or persons to whom said minor shall be apprenticed shall be a suitable person to have the charge and care of said minor, and fully to protect the interest of said minor. The said court shall require the said master or mistress to execute bond and security, payable to the State of Mississippi, conditioned that he or she shall furnish said minor with sufficient food and clothing; to treat said minor humanely; furnish medical attention in case of sickness; teach, or cause to be taught, him or her to read and write. if under fifteen years old, and will conform to any law that may be hereafter passed for the regulation of the duties and relation of master and apprentice.

Sec.3. In the management and control of said apprentice, said master or mistress shall have the Dower to inflict such moderate corporal chastisement as a father or guardian is allowed to inflict on his or her child or ward at common law: Provided, that in no case shall cruel or inhuman punishment be inflicted.

Sec. 4. If any apprentice shall leave the employment of his or her master or mistress, without his or her consent, said master or mistress may pursue and recapture said apprentice, and bring him or her before any justice of the peace of the county, whose duty it shall be to remand said apprentice to the service of his or her master or mistress; and in the (b) Mississippi, 1865 event of a refusal on the part of said apprentice so to return, then said justice shall commit said apprentice to the jail of said county, on failure to give bond, to the next term of the county court; and it shall be the duty of said court at the first term thereafter to investigate said case, and if the court shall be of opinion that said apprentice left the employment of his or her master or mistress without good cause, to order him or her to be punished, as provided for the punishment of hired freedmen, as may be from time to time provided for by law for desertion, until he or she shall agree to return to the service of his or her master or mistress:....if the court shall believe that said apprentice had good cause to quit his said master or mistress, the court shall discharge said apprentice from said indenture, and also enter a judgment against the master or mistress for not more than one hundred dollars, for the use and benefit of said apprentice.

Appendix F

Ratification Table for the 13th Amendment

The 38th Congress of the United States of America proposed the 13th Amendment to the Constitution of the United States to the legislatures of the several states on January 31, 1865. The ratification process was completed on December 6, 1865.

STATE	DATE RATIFIED	REJECTION DATE
Illinois	February 1, 1865	Not Applicable
Rhode Island	February 2, 1865	Not Applicable
Michigan	February 2, 1865	Not Applicable
Maryland	February 3, 1865	Not Applicable
New York	February 3, 1865	Not Applicable
Pennsylvania	February 3, 1865	Not Applicable
West Virginia	February 3, 1865	Not Applicable
Missouri	February 6, 1865	Not Applicable
Maine	February 7, 1865	Not Applicable
Kansas	February 7, 1865	Not Applicable
Massachusetts	February 7, 1865	Not Applicable
Virginia	February 9, 1865	Not Applicable
Ohio	February 10, 1865	Not Applicable
Indiana	February 13, 1865	Not Applicable
Nevada	February 16, 1865	Not Applicable

STATE	DATE RATIFIED	REJECTION DATE
Louisiana	February 17, 1865	Not Applicable
Minnesota	February 23, 1865	Not Applicable
Vermont	March 9, 1865	Not Applicable
Tennessee	April 7, 1865	Not Applicable
Arkansas	April 14, 1865	Not Applicable
Connecticut	May 4, 1865	Not Applicable
New Hampshire	July 1, 1865	Not Applicable
South Carolina	November 13, 1865	Not Applicable
Alabama	December 2, 1865	Not Applicable
North Carolina	December 4, 1865	Not Applicable
Georgia	December 6, 1865	Not Applicable
Oregon	December 8, 1865	Not Applicable
California	December 19, 1865	Not Applicable
Florida	December 28, 1865	Not Applicable
Iowa	January 15, 1866	Not Applicable
New Jersey	January 23, 1866	March 16, 1865
Texas	February 18, 1870	Not Applicable
Delaware	February 12, 1901	February 8, 1865
Kentucky	March 18, 1976	February 24, 1865
Mississippi	Not Applicable	December 4, 1865

Ratification Table for the 14th Amendment

The 39th Congress of the United States of America proposed the 14th Amendment to the Constitution of the United States to the legislatures of the several states on June 13, 1866. The ratification process was completed on July 9, 1868.[*]

STATE	DATE RATIFIED	REJECTION DATE
Connecticut	June 25, 1866	Not Applicable
New Jersey	November 12, 1980[*]	March 24, 1868
Oregon	September 1866	October 15, 1868
Vermont	October 30, 1866	Not Applicable
Ohio	January 4, 1867	January 15, 1868
New York	January 10, 1867	Not Applicable
Kansas	January 11, 1867	Not Applicable
Illinois	January 15, 1867	Not Applicable
West Virginia	January 16, 1867	Not Applicable
Minnesota	January 16, 1867	Not Applicable
Maine	January 19, 1867	Not Applicable
Nevada	January 22, 1867	Not Applicable
Indiana	January 23, 1867	Not Applicable
Missouri	January 25, 1867	Not Applicable
Rhode Island	February 7, 1867	Not Applicable

---

[*] On September 11, 1866, New Jersey's legislature voted to ratify the 14th Amendment. On March 24, 1868, it rescinded its pro-14th Amendment vote.

STATE	DATE RATIFIED	REJECTION DATE
Wisconsin	February 7, 1867	Not Applicable
Pennsylvania	February 12, 1867	Not Applicable
Massachusetts	March 20, 1867	Not Applicable
Nebraska	June 15, 1867	Not Applicable
Iowa	March 16, 1868	Not Applicable
Arkansas	April 6, 1868	Not Applicable
Florida	June 9, 1868	Not Applicable
North Carolina	July 4, 1868	**December 14, 1866**
Louisiana	July 9, 1868	**February 6, 1867**
South Carolina	July 9, 1868	**December 20, 1866**
Alabama	July 13, 1868	Not Applicable
Georgia	July 21, 1868	November 9, 1866
Virginia	October 8, 1869	January 9, 1867
Mississippi	January 17, 1870	Not Applicable
Texas	February 18, 1870	October 27, 1866
Delaware	February 12, 1901	February 8, 1867
Maryland	April 4, 1959	March 23, 1867
California	May 6, 1959	Not Applicable
Kentucky	March 6, 1976	January 8, 1967

Ratification Table for the 15th Amendment

The 40th Congress of the United States of America proposed the 15h Amendment to the Constitution of the United States to the legislatures of the several states on February 26, 1867. The ratification process was completed on February 3, 1870.

STATE	DATE RATIFIED	REJECTION DATE
Nevada	March 1, 1869	Not Applicable
West Virginia	March 3, 1869	Not Applicable
Illinois	March 5, 1869	Not Applicable
Louisiana	March 5, 1869	Not Applicable
North Carolina	March 5, 1869	Not Applicable
Michigan	March 8, 1869	Not Applicable
Wisconsin	March 9, 1869	Not Applicable
Maine	March 11, 1869	Not Applicable
Massachusetts	March 12, 1869	Not Applicable
Arkansas	March 15, 1869	Not Applicable
South Carolina	March 15, 1869	Not Applicable
Pennsylvania	March 25, 1869	Not Applicable
New York	April 14, 1869	January 5, 1870[*]
Indiana	May 14, 1869	Not Applicable
Connecticut	May 19, 1869	Not Applicable
Florida	June 14, 1869	Not Applicable

---

[*] New York's legislature ratified the 15th Amendment on March 30, 1870.

STATE	DATE RATIFIED	REJECTION DATE
New Hampshire	July 1, 1869	Not Applicable
Virginia	October 8, 1869	Not Applicable
Vermont	October 20, 1869	Not Applicable
Missouri	January 7, 1870	Not Applicable
Minnesota	January 13, 1870	Not Applicable
Mississippi	January 17, 1870	Not Applicable
Rhode Island	January 18, 1870	Not Applicable
Kansas	January 27, 1870	Not Applicable
Ohio	January 27, 1870	April 30, 1869
Georgia	February 2, 1870	Not Applicable
Iowa	February 3, 1870	Not Applicable
Nebraska	February 17, 1870	Not Applicable
Texas	February 18, 1870	Not Applicable
New Jersey	February 15, 1871	February 7, 1870
Delaware	February 12, 1901	March 18, 1869
Oregon	February 24, 1959	Not Applicable
California	April 3, 1962	January 28, 1870
Kentucky	March 18, 1976	March 12, 1869
Maryland	May 7, 1973	February 26, 1870
Tennessee	Not Applicable	February 16, 1869

Appendix G

**DATE: 02-09-1995
THE WHITE HOUSE
Office of the Press Secretary**

For Immediate Release **February 9, 1995**
EXECUTIVE ORDER 12949
- - - - - - -
FOREIGN INTELLIGENCE PHYSICAL SEARCHES

By the authority vested in me as President by the Constitution and the laws of the United States, including sections 302 and 303 of the Foreign Intelligence Surveillance Act of 1978 ("Act") (50 U.S.C. 1801, et seq.), as amended by Public Law 103- 359, and in order to provide for the authorization of physical searches for foreign intelligence purposes as set forth in the Act, it is hereby ordered as follows:

Section 1. Pursuant to section 302(a)(1) of the Act, the Attorney General is authorized to approve physical searches, without a court order, to acquire foreign intelligence information for periods of up to one year, if the Attorney General makes the certifications required by that section.

Sec. 2. Pursuant to section 302(b) of the Act,

the Attorney General is authorized to approve applications to the Foreign Intelligence Surveillance Court under section 303 of the Act to obtain orders for physical searches for the purpose of collecting foreign intelligence information.

Sec. 3. Pursuant to section 303(a)(7) of the Act, the following officials, each of whom is employed in the area of national security or defense, is designated to make the certifications required by section 303(a)(7) of the Act in support of applications to conduct physical searches:

(a) Secretary of State;

(b) Secretary of Defense;

(c) Director of Central Intelligence;

(d) Director of the Federal Bureau of Investigation;

(e) Deputy Secretary of State;

(f) Deputy Secretary of Defense; and

(g) Deputy Director of Central Intelligence.

None of the above officials, nor anyone officially acting in that capacity, may exercise the authority to make the above certifications, unless that official has been appointed by the President, by and with the advice and consent of the Senate.

WILLIAM J. CLINTON
THE WHITE HOUSE,
February 9, 1995.

About the Author

Pastor Michael S. Williams, D.Min. Is a native of San Francisco, California. He is a product of San Francisco's public school system. He received his **Bachelor of Arts** degree *cum laude*, from **Bishop College**, formerly of Dallas, Texas, in 1976. He earned the **Masters of Divinity and Doctor of Ministry** degrees from the world-renown **Pacific School of Religion**, Berkeley, California in 1979 and 1996 respectively.

Professional/Fraternal Activities

He served as the **Assistant to the President of the Graduate Theological Union from 1996-1997** and holds dual membership with the **American Academy of Religion** and the **Society of Biblical Literature**. Dr. Williams holds the rank of **Professor of Biblical Studies and Vice President for Development at the Southern Marin Bible Institute**. Dr. Williams is a member of **Alpha Phi Alpha, Inc.**

Denominational Activities

Dr. Williams has been in parish ministry for over a quarter century. He is a respected leader within his denomination, the **National Baptist Convention, USA, Inc.** He is a certified instructor through the **National Baptist Convention's (USA, Inc.) Department of Christian Education.** He served in a variety of pastoral and staff positions within the **United Methodist Church**, the **African Methodist Episcopal Zion Church**, the **National Baptist Convention of America**, and the **National Baptist Convention, USA, Inc.** Since 1989, Dr. Williams has served as **Pastor of the Saint James Missionary Baptist Church of San Francisco.** He served as the **Moderator of the Bay Area Baptist District Association (1995-99).**

Published Writings by Dr. Williams

"The Book of Job as a Reflection on the Practice of Ministry" *The Journal of Religious Thought* 54:2/55:1 (2000): 53-59

Sermon entitled, "Holding Up Your End" (*The African American Pulpit*, Summer 2000 Issue, Judson Press): 81-86.

If You Want to go to the Left, Then I'll Go to the Right, If You want to Go to the Right, Then, I'll Go to the Left: A Church Member's Guide to Conflict Resolution, 1999.

Some Thoughts For The Journey To Cana: Christian Matrimony: Choice Or Chance, 1998

From Eden to Egypt: The Book of Genesis Revisited. 1999

No Rights and No Respect: A Documentary Commentary on African Life in America, 2000

Twisting in the Wind: The Anglo-American Legal Tradition and ***AFRICANS*** *In America*, 2001

The Juneteenth Publishing Group published all of Dr. Williams's writings, with the exception of his journal publications.

Family

Since 1984, Pastor Williams has been married to the former Patricia A. Andrews. They are the parents of two children, Marthaa and Timothy.

www.ingramcontent.com/pod-product-compliance
Lightning Source LLC
Chambersburg PA
CBHW062027220426
43662CB00010B/1504